Open-mindedness and Education

Open-mindedness and Education

William Hare

William Hare

McGill-Queen's University Press

KINGSTON AND MONTREAL

© McGill-Queen's University Press 1979
Reprinted in paperback 1983
ISBN 0-7735-0345-5 (cloth)
ISBN 0-7735-0411-7 (paper)
Legal deposit third quarter 1979
Bibliothèque nationale du Québec

Design by H. Petersen-Wills
Printed in Canada

This book has been published with the help of
a grant from the Social Science Federation
of Canada, using funds provided by the Social
Sciences and Humanities Research Council of
Canada

To Niki, Andrew,
Antony, and Stephen

This, dear Crito, is the voice which I
seem to hear murmuring in my ears, like
the sound of the flute in the ears of the
mystic; that voice, I say, is humming in
my ears, and prevents me from hearing any
other. And I know that anything more
which you may say will be vain. Yet speak,
if you have anything to say.

SOCRATES

Open-mindedness is a quality which will
always exist where desire for knowledge
is genuine.

BERTRAND RUSSELL

Contents

Preface

This book attempts to demonstrate the meaning, possibility, and desirability of the attitude of open-mindedness, an attitude which, I believe, it is essential for education to promote. It is hoped that the arguments will be of interest to philosophers, educational theorists, and teachers in particular, but also to a nonspecialist audience. Accordingly, I have kept the use of technical language to a minimum.

In the detailed analyses of the concept of education which have appeared in the past fifteen years, much has been said about the centrality of knowledge and understanding in our idea of what it means to be an educated person. There have been vigorous disputes concerning the kind and extent of knowledge demanded if the concept of education is to be applicable. Is it, for example, the case that a person must have some acquaintance with all the major forms of knowledge? Or again, is the notion of a trained individual clearly distinct from that of an educated person? Very little has been said, however, about the attitude or attitudes which it might be necessary for the educated person to have with respect to the claims to knowledge which he makes, or to that which he claims to understand.

It is argued here that the appropriate attitude is that of open-mindedness, a term which readily appears in commencement exercises and popular addresses but less often in the more measured tones of philosophy. This neglect by philosophers is somewhat surprising in view of the vast amount of work on the concept of indoctrination, for to be indoctrinated is to have a closed mind. One would think that it would be worth spelling out what is involved in the positive attitude of open-mindedness.

This neglect may be due to a variety of factors. It may be, for example, that some writers have believed that in providing an analysis of some other term, such as neutrality (and there is a wealth of literature on this topic), that they were *ipso facto* providing an analysis of open-mindedness. I will be showing in this book that such a view is quite mistaken. On the other hand, it may have been thought that the concept is relatively noncontroversial and does not require analysis. Indeed, in the course of many discussions about this concept with other philosophers, I have found general agreement with the essential analysis of the concept in terms of a willingness to revise and reconsider one's views.

Still, I believe that it is necessary now to argue this point in detail because the idea of open-mindedness has become enmeshed in statements of educational theories and ideologies in which the essential analysis is ignored or denied and other, quite erroneous, interpretations are offered. Some of these are proving to be enormously influential on educational practice, and thus if mistaken models are to be avoided, it becomes important from the practical standpoint to clarify the concept.

There are, of course, many ways in which we can lose sight of the essential meaning of a concept which we once understood, and even now can understand if we could tear ourselves away from misleading suggestions. We may, for example, fall victim to some persuasive or stipulative definition, perhaps because the proposed definition states an educational principle to which we subscribe. This force may be at work in the definition in terms of neutrality. Secondly, contingently related features may come to be built into the very concept itself in the way in which freedom of the press has come to be thought of as part of the *meaning* of democracy. Thus if members of a certain group are found regularly to have closed minds, we will find before long that part of the meaning of open-mindedness is held to be that the person said to have this attitude does *not* belong to such a group. Again, even if we start out with the idea of a willingness to revise one's views as central to our understanding of open-mindedness, our inability or unwillingness to see *how* a person could fail to revise his view in the light of a certain objection can lead to the conclusion that anyone maintaining such a view must be closed-minded. It may be too that we move directly from *conceptual* considerations to *procedural* principles, for example from the concept of discussion to discussion as a teaching method, and refuse to allow the possibility that other methods might also represent an open-minded approach.

My purpose in this book is to illustrate that these and other traps have *in fact* been at work in educational theory, and have even succeeded in tripping up those philosophers who have briefly commented on open-mindedness. A careful review of relevant educational literature shows that open-mindedness is a much misunderstood notion and that a careful study of the idea is needed if it is to serve as an educational aim, as I believe it should.

I have tried wherever possible to refer to relevant empirical work. My concern has been to show the importance of distinguishing conceptual and empirical issues, and to indicate that open-mindedness cannot seriously be pursued unless both conceptual and empirical work is undertaken. Recently there has developed a general dissatisfaction with the results of several decades' research on teaching effectiveness and a call has been issued for a "reconceptualization of the entire problem."[1] This book is devoted to a re-examination of one concept which is regularly claimed to be promoted more effectively by one method of teaching rather than another, in order that those who wish to pursue this empirical issue may have a more serviceable tool to work with. Similarly, unless we have a firm understanding of the concept of open-mindedness, we will not be in a position to assess, for example, the claim that one of the major results of attending college or university is the development of open-mindedness in the student.[2]

I am very grateful to Alan White who read and criticized each part of this book as it came along, and to David Braybrooke who commented on a number of earlier papers out of which the ideas for the book developed. Earlier versions of certain parts of the argument in chapters 3, 6, and 7 have appeared in articles in *The Journal of Educational Thought, Kansas Studies in Education, Agora,* and *Teaching Politics.* I am grateful to the editors of these journals for allowing me to draw upon these papers. Andrew Bjerring made valuable criticisms of a version of chapter 3 presented at the annual meeting of the Canadian Society for the Study of Education in June 1978, and the two anonymous referees appointed by the Social Science Federation of Canada offered useful suggestions which led me to make several revisions. I wish to thank the Federation for its support in aid of publication and for the courtesy and efficiency shown at each stage of the review process. This is also the place to record my general indebtedness to James Gribble and Jonas Soltis for their help and encouragement over the years. Dalhousie University very generously granted me sabbatical leave in 1976-77 which permitted me to undertake this study, and I was further supported at that time by a Canada Council Leave Fellowship. My thanks to Mrs. Linda MacDonald who typed the manuscript with accuracy, and to Mrs. Hazel Waters and Mrs. Rose Pritzker for additional secretarial assistance. I could not have succeeded in carrying this project through to completion without the support, advice, and interest of my wife, Niki.

As this book was going to press, I learned with deep regret of the death of Dr. Robert Jackson, head of the Ontario Royal Commission on Declining School Enrolments.

William Hare
Dalhousie University

The concept of open-mindedness

1

1/ Preliminary remarks

Among the parasynthetic formations in English, which include such types as "good-natured," "wrong-headed," and
"quick-witted," there is a fairly small but important group
which combines various adjectives with the past participle of
"mind" to produce participial adjectives of the form "φ-
minded." A list of the more common words in this group
would include: narrow-, broad-, (cf. small-, large-), quick-,
simple-, fair-, foul-, evil-, noble-, healthy-, bloody-, single-,
weak-, (cf. tender), tough-, feeble-, absent-, independent-, and
the one of special interest here, open-minded. There appear to
be no logical reasons why some other adjectives have not been
formed in this manner. For example, we do not find "deep-
minded," though a person can be described as being deep.
Similarly, we do not always find the antonym of those adjectives which we do have. Thus we have "simple-minded" but
not "complex-minded," "independent-," but not "depen-
dent-minded." Even "closed-minded" which sometimes can
be found is not nearly as common as "open-minded." We
tend rather to say that A has a closed mind. But it is perhaps
the awkwardness in speech produced by the repetition of the

letter "d" which in the latter case accounts for this and not any conceptual reason. Presumably, then, some formations just catch on and become fashionable, while others do not. Hume, for example, referred to "greatness of mind" (one of those qualities which is immediately agreeable to the one who has it), by which he meant something close to "noble-minded" and "dignified."[1] We can still use the adjective "great" in context to capture this sense, but "great-minded" did not enter our language. Here again, there were no conceptual difficulties, but possibly the existence of "noble-minded" made other formations here redundant. These are, however, speculations in the history of language development and can safely be left to others more qualified. Suffice it to say that "open-mindedness," for whatever reason, appears to have been a relative late-comer. The O.E.D. (1908) does not appear to list it, though it does refer to the expression to "open one's mind or heart."[2] The term then is relatively new, but the idea captured by it is not at all new, as I will show as the concept is analysed.

2/ "ϕ-minded"

What this group of adjectives has in common is that they are all employed to comment in some way on a person's *thinking*. But it is important to notice at once that (a) the *sort* of comment being made is not always the same and (b) *what* it is about our thinking which is being commented on also varies.

(a) The sort of comment

(i) It is obvious that some of these words can be used to commend and others to condemn; still others can be used in either way. And in this, as Hume aptly put it, "the very nature of language guides us almost infallibly."[3] Thus we are in no doubt at all how to take such ascriptions as evil-, fair-, foul-, bloody-, noble-, weak-, feeble-, narrow-minded. Open-minded carries generally *favourable* overtones, though it will be worth asking later if it invariably does so. Sometimes the one word can be used in commendatory *and* condemnatory fashion. Thus simple-minded can be used to condemn A as naïve or foolish, or it may be used to laud A for rejecting pretentious sophistication. The great majority then are used in *assessment*, and even those such as "single-minded" which may be used descriptively, typically suggest an evaluation, in this case, favourable.

(ii) Secondly, we should notice that the commendation or condemnation is, with some words, intellectual, but with others, moral; while a few terms manage to suggest both at once. Fair-, evil-, noble-, bloody-, healthy-minded all tend to involve *moral* assessment. Weak-, independent-, absent-, feeble-, simple-, quick-, and open-minded tend to involve *intellectual* assessment. (I will consider later ways in which such intellectual comments might also provoke moral comments in particular cases, e.g., the teacher who fails to be open-minded.) Some like narrow-, broad-minded seem to involve both intellectual and moral comment. (I have not found any such adjectives which primarily make assessments of personality[4] and this is perhaps because personality assessments involve the reactions of others to a person's behaviour, manner, etc., quite apart from any reference to his intentions or awareness. If A is trying to be amusing, he may yet be very dull. He may indeed have a lively mind, but be unable to communicate this in his manner. Dull and dim-witted are quite different.)

(iii) Sometimes such words are used to ascribe *traits* of intellect or *traits* of moral character, i.e., how people tend to think *in certain circumstances*. To say that A *is* ϕ-minded is to say, normally, that his thinking has tended to be characterized in this way in the past and is liable to be so characterized in future.[5] Of course, the limitation *in certain circumstances* is important because A may be ϕ-minded in some areas or ways and not in others. On the other hand, if A is a ϕ-*minded person*, we would insist that there be no major counter-example to this in any area of his life.

A trait ascription is not necessarily involved, however, for if A is ϕ-minded he may yet act in a way which is contradictory of this. Thus A who has a closed mind generally (trait-ascription) may on a given occasion act in a way which can only be described as open-minded. But this single act does not earn him the trait-ascription. If we say, "A is open-minded," we are ascribing a trait, whereas if we say, "A acted open-mindedly" or "A acted in an open-minded way" or even "that was open-minded of A," we are commenting on a particular instance, and a trait ascription may not be involved.

Thus, to summarize, the *sort* of comment being made may be favourable or unfavourable; an intellectual or a moral assessment, a trait ascription or an isolated single comment.

(b) What is being commented on
(i) It is important that we bear in mind here that "thinking" is used in a number of distinct, albeit related, ways in English.[6] For our purposes the relevant senses are: (1) the *result* sense, thinking *of* things; (2) the *possession* of an opinion, etc.; (3) the *activity* of thinking. That these are different is shown by the following considerations:
(1) When a person thinks of a word, for example, it is not implied (still less does it *mean*) that he has some opinion about this word. Again, the word may just pop into his mind though he had not been trying to think of it. (2) To think that something is the case is not to be engaged in the activity of thinking—it is true that I think that philosophy is interesting even when I am fast asleep. Similarly, I can think that something is so, though I am not now thinking of it. (3) Finally, I can be thinking what the answer is without thinking of the answer and without thinking the answer is such and such. Thus there are at least three aspects to the complex notion of "thinking."
(ii) We need now to ask *which* of these aspects our various adjectives qualify. There are seven possibilities. A word "φ-minded" could qualify (1) the result sense, (2) the activity *and* result senses, (3) the possession *and* result

senses, (4) the activity sense, (5) the possession *and* activity senses, (6) the possession sense, (7) all three senses. Let us consider the possibilities:

(1)   Quick-mindedness is the name of an ability which some people have and others do not. The individual who is quick-minded tends to be able to call names, dates, formulae, arguments, etc., readily to mind. We use this term of people whose memories and wits are sharp. The person so described is good at *thinking of* certain things when he wants or needs to think of them. When we say, "that was quick-minded of A," we mean to comment on his thinking of something. Quick-mindedness is the *ability to think of* things. Thus, although the term does not directly qualify the result itself since it qualifies the *ability to get results*, it is nevertheless more closely tied to the result sense than to the other senses of thinking. For example, the opinion a man possesses could not in itself be described as quick-minded, even though his ability to think rapidly of an opinion might be. In this latter case again it is the getting hold of certain results which is central. Nor does the term qualify the *way* in which we set about the task of thinking of things, hence it does not qualify the activity sense.

(2)   Feeble-minded, however, is related to the result sense *and* the activity sense. It is first the name of a lack of a certain ability, as in the case of an old person or a sick person who cannot *think of*, say, his own son's name. But also the term will be used of someone who cannot *follow* a simple narrative or film and thus it is a term which also has application to a person's activities in thinking about things. By contrast the opinion we possess cannot itself be called feeble-minded and the mere possession of an opinion does not mean that A is feeble-minded. This is the case even though A's feeble-mindedness may explain why he has certain opinions or has no opinion on something.

(3)   I can think of no term of this type which can qualify both result and possession senses. *A fortiori* then (7) must also be a null class.

(4)   An example of a term which chiefly relates to the activity of thinking is independent-minded. A is independent-minded if he *tends* to make up his own mind and in general acts autonomously. Of course, a tendency is not an activity, but the point here is that *what* it is that A has a tendency to do is to engage in thinking of a certain sort or in a certain way, rather than a tendency to *hold* opinions of a certain sort. It is in this way that independent-minded is said to relate to the *activity* sense rather than to the *possession* sense. Similarly, the result sense is not involved, for independent-minded does not qualify our ability to think of certain things.

(5)   A term such as fair-minded basically applies to the activity of thinking for it tells us that the person in question sets about an inquiry in a certain way. For example, he tried to be impartial and without prejudice. Of course, a verdict could turn out to be fair even though the jury did not set about their task in a *fair-minded* way. Still, I think we sometimes find "fair" being replaced by "fair-minded" with opinions, judgments, verdicts and so on, such that the term has come to apply by extension to the possession sense also. What was originally a *manifestation* of fair-mindedness is now said to be fair-minded itself. Perhaps a clearer case is simple-minded. An approach to a problem (i.e., one's activity) can properly be called simple-minded. Suppose, for example, that in analysing a concept, a philosopher were to base everything on etymological considerations (as Dewey is reputed to have done in claiming that indoctrination merely meant teaching). This *approach* would certainly be called simple-minded, but also the *belief* or *opinion* that one could base analysis on etymology alone would be said to be simple-minded. A is simple-minded to the extent that he holds views such as these and/or to the extent that he approaches problems in a certain way.

(6)   A term such as narrow-minded seems to apply mainly to the possession sense, A is narrow-minded if he holds certain views and opinions. Narrow-minded-

ness applies to one who fails to extend the same judgment to X which he extends to Y because X belongs to some other class, when that difference is not relevant. Thus those who base policies on criteria such as skin colour, are properly said to be narrow-minded insofar as this criterion is irrelevant to the issue. It often takes the form of believing that whatever falls outside one's own culture, group, or class, cannot be good, and thus it is literally a very *restricted* or *narrow* set of beliefs which is approved. It is not always carefully distinguished from having a closed mind in ordinary usage, but I will argue that open-mindedness and its contrast do not relate to the possession of certain beliefs but rather to the way in which those beliefs are held. Thus it will appear that although A has a narrow mind, he may not have a closed mind, i.e., the one does not entail the other.

In the ascription of these terms reference to *context* is important. It is quick-minded of a seven-year-old to think of something but not necessarily so of an adult. A view may come to be thought of as simple-minded in the light of new research, but this does not mean that it was simple-minded when originally propounded. (Contrast here comments above about its truth or falsity. If the theory is false, it will always be false, though it might have appeared to be true and could have been universally accepted.) Thus the relevant context can involve different factors, such as the person's level of development, or available knowledge. Sometimes it relates to the individual's intention as, for example, when literary critics argue against would-be censors that a novelist's remark must not be considered *out of context* if it is to be assessed as foul-minded or not.

3/ Open-minded

What aspect of thinking is qualified when a person is called "open-minded"? We can begin by distinguishing two ways in which a person may fail to be open-minded. (i) If A is subjected to an intense program of indoctrination, he may become quite *incapable* of thinking of any objections to his own position, or of recognizing any merit in contrary points of view. His mind is closed to alternatives because he is unable to entertain them. (ii) On the other hand, B may be perfectly *able* to think of difficulties in his position but try to ignore them. He may be able to recognize a good counter-argument, but be *unwilling* to attend to such arguments.

In either of these ways, an individual can manifest a closed mind. It is tempting at first to move to the positive view that if a person is willing to entertain objections, is prepared to revise his position and so on, that he is open-minded. But it seems possible that a person who has been indoctrinated could be unaware of his inability to give serious consideration to the positions which others maintain, and could be willing to entertain criticisms of his own views. If a person knows that an action of a certain sort, e.g., translating from a foreign language, is beyond him, he will be neither willing nor unwilling to do it. Quite simply, he *cannot* do it. But if we do not recognize that we cannot do something, it makes sense to say that we are willing. Hence it seems that we must say that a person must be both willing *and* able to revise his own position if he is to be open-minded. We must bear in mind further that there are cases in which a person deceives himself into thinking that he is willing to revise his opinions when he is not in fact prepared to do this.

If a person fails to think of an objection to his own position, it does not, of course, follow that he is not open-minded, for many factors can explain why he does not do so. An individual may well examine his views critically without succeeding in thinking of any objections to them. We do not want to make imagination, cleverness, or creativity necessary conditions of open-mindedness. Thus it is not the case that the ability to get results is a necessary condition of open-mindedness, but it is necessary that the person should not have been made incapable of the activity of giving consideration to such objections as others raise.

A person who is open-minded is disposed to revise or reject the position he holds if sound objections are brought against it, or, in the situation in which the person presently has no opinion on some issue, he is disposed to make up his mind in the light of available evidence and argument as objectively and as impartially as possible. If a person adopts an opinion because it is the prescribed party line, or if he thinks of an objection to his position but quietly ignores it, or if he sets himself to give attention only to those findings which support his own case, he fails in each case to be open-minded. He must rather be disposed to form and revise his views in the light of evidence and argument.[7] As the discussion in chapter 2 will reveal, we may adopt the attitude of open-mindedness with respect to highly particularized and specific beliefs or to more general and wide-ranging hypotheses, theories, and conceptual frameworks. The *object* of one's open-mindedness varies, but the *meaning* of open-mindedness remains constant. Again a variety of criteria can indicate the presence or absence of open-mindedness but what is present or absent is one and the same in each case. For example, there are numerous ways, such as refusing to look at or listen to something, failing to consider a point, ignoring an opponent, etc., in which a person can indicate that he has a closed mind; but these different actions tell us the same thing, that is, that he is not disposed to revise the view he holds in the light of evidence and argument. Often, too, there may be no actual objection to consider, but in saying that the person is open-minded, we reveal our assessment of how we think the person *would* act should objections be raised to his view. He would give attention to the objections, he would make revisions in a certain context, he would give up a view altogether. In short, we judge that he is disposed to reconsider.

Let us look at a case in which the criteria which indicate open-mindedness might be tighter or more strict than other cases, for this will serve to illustrate both the fact that the criteria are various and that the meaning is constant. Sometimes an individual is not merely willing to *look at* counter-arguments which others may produce, he is in addition ready to *look for* weaknesses in his own position. This was the "utterly different" attitude which the young Popper detected in Einstein and which so impressed him.[8] It is apparently rare, if we can credit reports which suggest that researchers often fail to follow up experiments which suggest a weakness in their own hypotheses. We need not claim that they consciously suppress or minimize certain findings but for whatever reason, they do not *in fact* actively seek out possible deficiencies in their theories.

In ordinary, nonscholarly contexts, we would not demand as a necessary condition of open-mindedness that the man in the street actively *look for* problems in his own general beliefs; it is enough that he is willing to consider such problems if they are brought to his attention. In other contexts, however, our criteria might be more strict. Of the researcher who is not prepared to seek out crucial tests for his hypotheses we would certainly say that we would *expect* (normative sense) him to be more open-minded, and in extreme cases we might be inclined to withhold the ascription altogether. An extreme case might be provided by the situation of a researcher who is himself uniquely capable of carrying out a certain test. This person can hardly protest that he is willing to evaluate the results when someone else has carried out the test. This tighter criterion is not logically implied by the very notion of research for our researcher could continue to earn this description (i.e. researcher) by doing other work. The criterion reflects our normative judgment of the attitude which is appropriate in a given context. If in a given context "open-minded researcher" implies that the person *seeks out* objections whereas in a given context "open-minded teacher" does not imply this, we cannot infer that the *meaning* of "open-minded" has shifted from one case to the other, for it is clear that the implication of a concept may vary from one context to another without the essential meaning changing.[9] And, as I have shown above, one's open-mindedness can take a variety of forms in different circumstances. It will be of some importance later, particularly in chapter 4, to bear in mind that these forms or ways in which we *can* display open-minded-ness do not *necessarily* show in every case that we are open-minded, any more than the fact that gardening can take a variety of forms including, for example, digging, shows that digging always constitutes gardening. To be digging a grave is not to be gardening. Open-mindedness can take the form of considering the views of our opponents, but that such an activity is not necessarily an instance of open-mindedness is a point which will be demonstrated later. It will always be necessary to ask if the observed action does indeed show a disposition to revise one's views or to form them appropriately, and this will involve, among other things, attention to the individual's purpose and motives.

The person subjected to a successful program of indoctrination, referred to at the outset of this section, will have a closed mind and be unable to think objectively and impartially though he may not realise this. He is *doomed* to fail in such "attempts" and is thus quite unlike the ordinary individual who may be always *liable* to fail to meet these standards because of unconscious prejudice. Insofar as the latter person strives to be objective and impartial, he will be properly said to be open-minded even though he should on occasion fall short of these standards. Thus the fact that a person's account of an event is biased in that it falls short of objectivity and impartiality does not entail that the account represents closed-mindedness. The person may indeed be willing to revise the account in the light of counter-argument, and come to admit that his original account was biased.

4/ Rationality

Open-mindedness is an aspect of being rational, but the two concepts are not synonymous. There are many ways in which a person may fail to be rational, and failing to be open-minded is just one such way. For example, a person may fall short of rationality by offering an argument which is invalid; let us say that he commits the fallacy of affirming the consequent. He asks that we accept that if p then q. Then he points out that

q. He concludes by affirming p. We, of course, will rightly charge that this is irrational, that it does not follow. But we are not at all entitled to say that he is not open-minded just because he has committed a fallacy. In the light of our reply, we may see at once that he is disposed to withdraw the argument. A person not very adept at logic might even *tend* to commit fallacies of this sort yet deserve the ascription open-minded on the basis of his disposition to withdraw such fallacious arguments when the flaw is pointed out.

In much the same way, accounts in science, history, and literary criticism may be irrational without being closed-minded. They may contain inconsistencies and contradictions, ambiguity and confusion, hasty and careless commentary, rash and simplistic generalizations, and numerous such faults against the canons of the discipline, without the author incurring the charge of closed-mindedness. Again the central question to be raised is that concerning the author's disposition or lack of it to revise, reconsider, and judge anew when the contradiction is unearthed, the hasty generalization challenged, or the simplistic view exposed.

Closed-mindedness is, however, *one* way of being irrational. We contrast a rational decision, for example, with one that is arbitrary, where the latter does not heed the demands of evidence and argument which the former strives to satisfy. An arbitrary judgment is passed in court if whim or the toss of a coin determines a man's guilt. The rational course is to try to uncover the relevant evidence which bears upon the charge in question. But the open-minded attitude is precisely that of being willing to form and revise our views in the light of relevant and pertinent considerations. The closed-minded individual is either not able to take account of counter-evidence which would upset his views because he is caught in the grip of an unshakable conviction, or has set himself to ignore and dismiss counter-evidence which would challenge his views. And it is his inability or unwillingness to follow reason where it leads which leads us to say that he fails to be rational.

If a person is applying some well-known theorem, for example in mathematics, he is trying to be rational insofar as he is trying to be consistent, accurate, logical, and so on. Often the question of his open-mindedness will not come up at all. If the theorem is well established and the application of it straightforward, the context of revision or second thoughts may be very far removed. Open-mindedness raises its head when, for example, the theorem or its application is criticized or challenged. Is the mathematician disposed to reconsider his views about the theorem or his application of it in the light of the criticism? If he fails in this task, then he fails of open-mindedness and falls short of being rational. Of course, it is not demanded that he *actually* revise his views. The criticisms may themselves be irrational and the one who offers them may be forced to revise his position.

Recently the head of Ontario's Royal Commission on Declining School Enrolments has come under heavy criticism in the Canadian media for certain remarks pertaining to Canadian immigration trends and patterns. If we are to be rational, however, we need to bear in mind relevant distinctions, and thus we must distinguish between our assessment of a person's *attitude* towards certain trends (always supposing that we are properly informed of what that attitude is) and our assessment of the claim that certain trends are *in fact* occurring. Now although, as we will see in more detail in chapter 5, it has become fashionable to call into question *all* the distinctions which we draw including that between descriptive and evaluative comments, there remains a difference between the claims (1) that X is happening and (2) that it is a good/bad thing that X is happening. We fall short of rationality if we ignore this distinction. But this is not *per se* to be closed-minded. The latter attitude surfaces when we set ourselves in advance to reject certain claims whatever the evidence. A good illustration of this occurs in a recent comment on the controversy in question. Noting that the Ontario commissioner has been retained to complete his report on declining enrolments, a writer to the *Toronto Star*, June 1, 1978, observes that "a commissioner who has lost his credibility is not going to have his findings acceptable to a majority of the population." But whether or not the findings are acceptable depends upon the facts which are documented and to decide in advance that they will be unacceptable is to preclude the possibility of having our judgment informed or revised in the light of forthcoming evidence. It is this disposition to reject the findings whatever the evidence may be which marks this as a case of closed-mindedness.

5/ Vagueness

Reflection on the latter point often leads to the general charge that an analysis in terms of a willingness to revise one's views in the light of relevant counter-evidence and argument is hopelessly vague. This general charge breaks down into specific complaints.

(a) Identifying the open-minded person
It is true, of course, as I noted in section 3, that a person may deceive himself into thinking that he is open-minded. Similarly, he may deceive others. He gives us to believe that he is *willing* to revise his beliefs and simply has not yet been convinced that they *need* to be revised, when in reality he is not willing at all to revise them. We may concede that this is a difficulty, but not one which casts doubt on the adequacy of the analysis. It is often the case that we know the meaning of a concept but have difficulty in attributing it to individuals. We know what it means for someone to be concerned, interested, sincere, and so on, but yet often ascribe such adjectives in error. It may happen too that there will arise serious disputes among reasonable people about who is to count as an open-minded person. But, as Antony Flew has convincingly argued in this connection,[10] what this shows is that there are bound to be conflicts over the application of certain terms (especially those which have a use in ideological controversy and a built-in evaluative component), and not that the analysis is faulty.

(b) The exact meaning of open-mindedness
There will perhaps be a temptation to ask when *exactly* we would expect the open-minded person to revise his views.

There is not, however, an exact answer to this question any more than there is an exact answer to the query when we would expect a person with a sense of humour to laugh. When open-mindedness is used to ascribe a trait, it describes, as do other trait names, the sorts of ways (not precise, mandatory ways, but an open-ended range of ways) in which people frequently (but not always and necessarily) behave in certain sorts (not precisely specified) of circumstances. A football player with good judgment is one who among other things can anticipate and intercept certain passes. But which ones exactly? At what precise speed and angle? There are no answers to these questions, and if we were to stipulate and invent answers, no football commentator could employ the exact new term we had devised. We would give up our imprecise but usefully vague current term for a new and exact one which would be of no use to us. Good judgment and anticipation, like a sense of humour and open-mindedness, is not an all-or-nothing affair. Acquisition of such qualities cannot normally be precisely, but only roughly, dated: we can film and clock the exact moment when, in being told an amazing story, a person becomes open-mouthed; but open-minded is not like this. You cannot be more or less dead or pregnant, but you can be more or less open-minded. There is not an exact border between closed and open-mindedness as there is between Canada and the U.S.A., but this does not mean that we cannot recognize and ascribe these traits, though it does, of course, imply that in some cases we will not know quite what to say. Vagueness is, of course, sometimes objectionable. A student can at a certain time reasonably demand to be told unequivocally whether he has passed or failed the class in question. But he cannot similarly demand to be told unequivocally what *exactly* he would have to do to earn on his philosophy paper the comment "good judgment shown." It is an advantage rather than a fault that language contains such usefully vague, though not at all meaningless, terms. In particular cases, we may be able to say, for example, that if a person does not change his view when presented with certain specific evidence he surely fails to be open-minded. But we cannot always or necessarily make such explicit claims.

6/   The alleged nonexistence
of the traditional virtues

The mistake criticized above is reflected, I believe, in contemporary educational theory in the widely-accepted critique of the so-called "bag of virtues" approach to moral education. This is the view that there are distinct virtues, such as honesty, self-control, a sense of responsibility, and so on, and that one part of moral education at least consists in encouraging the development of such virtues. Laurence Kohlberg, who has championed the rejection of such a conception of moral education, writes that "the psychologist's objection to the bag of virtues is that there is no such thing."[11] If I understand Kohlberg's reasons for this conclusion, they rest at bottom on a misunderstanding of the logic of trait-names. He points out, following the findings of Hartshorne and May,[12] that "almost everyone cheats some of the time," that "if a person cheats in one situation, it does not mean he will or will not cheat in another," and that "people who cheat express as much or more moral disapproval of cheating as those who do not cheat."[13] But none of these findings has any tendency to show that the "bag of virtues" is a myth. As we have seen, people may readily deceive themselves into thinking that they are open-minded, and it is easy to see how they might then condemn closed-mindedness. The fact that almost all people cheat at some time, and that those who will not cheat in certain areas will cheat in others, does not show that the trait cannot be applied to some people more appropriately than to others. Traits, after all, describe the ways in which people *tend* to act, and these tendencies can vary markedly from one person to another, even if counter-instances to the tendency can be found in each case. Moreover, even if X cheats in certain cases only, we can still properly ascribe the trait, with appropriate qualifications.

Similarly, we should resist any attempt to dismiss open-mindedness as being a member of a nonexistent bag of intellectual virtues. We can admit, what is no doubt true, that all of us are closed-minded at some moments and in certain areas, and that we are capable of verbally supporting open-mindedness while in reality being closed-minded. But we may act on occasion in ways which are inconsistent with any specific trait without the trait being withdrawn. To tend to do something is not always or necessarily to do it. There is no reason too why we could not be open-minded about very many issues yet closed-minded in a particular area, for the trait need not be ascribed to our thinking in *every* area. Open-mindedness is not the name of an all-or-nothing state. It states rather that a person is characteristically inclined to think in a certain way, and the fact that a person is characteristically inclined to be open-minded does not preclude the possibility that at times we will want to say "that was closed-minded of him."[14]

7/ The limits of open-mindedness

Let us ask finally here if we are to impose any limits on the general claim that an open-minded person is one who is willing and able to revise his beliefs. Consider, for example, the different situation of the man in the dock and the person on the jury with respect to the charge that the former is guilty. We expect (normative sense) the juror to be open-minded as he listens to the evidence. He should be willing to revise an early view that the man is guilty if a striking piece of evidence, showing the man to be innocent, turns up. But how is the accused to be open-minded about the charge? If he is innocent then normally he knows that he is innocent, and we cannot urge him to be willing to revise his belief. The only room for open-mindedness on his part would appear if the prosecution were able to produce some reason to believe that, for example, the man had suffered a loss of memory about the incident. But if the man has no reason to suspect such extraordinary hypotheses,[15] and has every reason to trust his own memory, then there is nothing for him to be open-minded about.

A willingness to revise certain logical principles cannot properly be demanded, because such principles are presupposed in the activity of being open-minded. As we have seen, we revise a belief we hold (if we are rational), when relevant reasons begin to appear showing the belief in question to be mistaken. Suppose, however, we ask if we can be open-minded about *the principle of revising beliefs in the light of relevant reasons*. The obvious difficulty here is that any attempt to adopt an open-minded attitude towards this would at once presuppose this principle, for we would merely state our willingness to give it up *in the light of relevant reasons*. To abandon it without good reason would not be open-minded but merely arbitrary. This principle is not one which the open-minded person can be disposed to revise, because in being open-minded the person is disposed among other things *to act on the principle*. It is invoked in any attempt at open-mindedness, hence it is itself not something one can sensibly claim to be open-minded about.

It is not, of course, for every slip into a contradiction, for example, that a person deserves to be called closed-minded. An open-minded person may well utter a self-contradiction yet be willing to withdraw it when it is pointed out. Contradiction and open-mindedness are not in this sense at odds. And yet, the avoidance of contradiction is a fundamental demand of rational inquiry. The occurrence of contradiction is just the sort of event which calls for revision of one's position. If a person had no sense of what a contradiction was, he would lack one of the essential elements in trying to be open-minded. To be open-minded is, among other things, to be willing to revise one's position if it is shown to lead to self-contradiction. Since this is part of one's disposition to be open-minded, it is not itself a proper object of the attitude of open-mindedness. It is only as a joke and a piece of sarcasm that we say of the person apparently willing to embrace a self-contradiction, "How very open-minded of him!" This is literally to carry the attitude to *absurd* lengths.

A scientific theory may state that if A exists then B exists. If we are to be open-minded here, the nonexistence of B forces us either to hold that A does not exist or to abandon the hypothesis concerned with A and B. We invoke the logical argument form:

(1) $p \supset q$
(2) $\sim q$
(3) $\sim p$

where p is said to imply q, q is found not to exist, and therefore p must be abandoned. To be willing to abandon the original hypothesis, is just to be willing to accept the implication of the counter-example (i.e. $\sim q$), where the consequent is denied. But what could it mean to be open-minded about this *argument-form*? Are we to suggest that it might turn out itself to be open to objection by way of counter-example? Clearly any attempt to take this line would presuppose the form of the argument itself and would thus be self-defeating. This form as such is an integral part of our notion of revisability and is not appropriately subject itself to the attitude.

In scientific research, on the other hand, the mere fact that we have every reason to believe, and no reason to doubt, a particular hypothesis does not impose any constraint on the attitude of open-mindedness. A scientist in the late nineteenth century may have had no reason to doubt Newton's theories. Still, it was possible and meaningful for such a scientist to assert that, although he did not think that the theory would be surpassed, he was quite willing to revise this view if the evidence were such as to justify a revision.

In summary then, (1) with respect to certain of our beliefs which we know to be correct, "open-mindedness" will be little more than a nod in the direction of scepticism—"I could be dreaming"; (2) with respect to certain logical principles, open-mindedness has no room to operate since such principles are themselves involved and invoked in the attitude; (3) but with theories and hypotheses in the disciplines, together with more specific beliefs, open-mindedness involves being disposed to revise or abandon such belief in the light of relevant counter-evidence and counter-argument, no matter how unlikely is thought to be the possibility of a serious challenge.

8/ Conclusion

It would seem then that the trait of open-mindedness qualifies a person's activities in thinking, chiefly his ability and willingness to form and revise his views in the light of evidence and argument. This will be unpacked into a variety of dispositions such as a willingness to consider objections, to subject his own views to critical scrutiny, to seek out objections to his own position, and so on. The context will determine which of these more specific criteria are demanded. Before we can be really confident, however, that this analysis is on the right lines, we must turn to examine rival analyses and definitions, notably those which associate open-mindedness with the content of a person's beliefs, or with the state of being neutral (or ignorant), or with the activity of doubting. These theories and claims will occupy us in chapter 2.

Alternative views of open-mindedness

2

1/ The content of one's beliefs

It is sometimes thought that open-mindedness is to be identified with having certain opinions, or that having certain opinions is a *necessary* or a *sufficient* condition of open-mindedness. People commonly say such things as "No open-minded person could believe that"[1] in which the possession of a certain belief is alleged to be a sufficient condition for denying that the person is open-minded. For example, in a letter in *The Guardian*, Oct. 21, 1976, with the heading "Closed Minds and Nuclear Options," the writer observes that his opponent "says he is unconvinced about fast reactors." The writer adds: "I think from his comments he is not open to being convinced." (The case would, of course, be different if instead of "from his comments" we had something like "from the attitude we detect behind his comments" or "from the spirit in which his comments were made.") This could be regarded as the view that *only if* a person rejects a certain belief (either believes that it is false or at least does not believe it) can he be said to be open-minded, i.e., a necessary condition of open-mindedness is asserted. It is significant, for example, that people are often unwilling to learn *how* an individual holds his beliefs but are anxious to silence him once they know (or think they know) *what* he believes. Again we hear comments such as "Well, if he believes that, then he is open-minded," where some belief is regarded as confirming that the person is open-minded. To say that the possession of certain opinions is *both* necessary and sufficient for open-mindedness is to say that these are equivalent. We can proceed then by showing that the possession of certain opinions is neither necessary nor sufficient for the trait ascription.

Let us consider first, however, an actual case in which the comments above are, in fact, often made. Suppose that A, in line with the recommendations of the *Report of the Royal Commission on Bilingualism and Biculturalism* (Ottawa, 1967), is of the opinion that, depending upon the concentration of the minority population, Canadian educational systems should recognize the right of parents to have their children educated in the official language of their choice. Suppose further that B is opposed to this recommendation and that C has not yet made up his mind on the question. Many in Canada would hold that this is enough to show that A is open-minded, that C may be open-minded, and that B is closed-minded. That is, it is widely held that being of A's opinion is a sufficient indication of open-mindedness and being of B's opinion enough to establish that one is closed-minded. Some go further and hold that, not only does A's position establish that he is open-minded, *only if* A's position is adopted can a person be open-minded on this matter. For this latter group then, open-mindedness has simply become *equivalent* to holding A's position. Others, however, take a somewhat weaker stand and allow, as I said above, that C too may be open-minded and thus do not demand that A's position be adopted if open-mindedness is to be ascribed. But those who sympathize with the neutral position often go beyond the correct point that C *may* be open-minded to hold either (i) that *unless* one is neutral, as C is, one cannot be open-minded, or (ii) that *if* one is neutral then one is open-minded. Those who hold *both* of the last-mentioned views take neutrality to be equivalent to open-mindedness. In practice, of course, the neutrality-is-open-mindedness group tend to restrict the application of the concept of open-mindedness to areas of controversy and dispute, a position which will be shown later to be false. Their mistake arises, I believe, largely because they base their analysis on a very limited selection of issues.

The correct view, I will argue, is that it is possible that A, B, and C are all equally open-minded. On the other hand, each one may have a closed mind. We cannot tell just by learning what their *view* is on this issue. All of the claims above, other than those which allow that A, B, or C *may* be open-minded, are false. I will also be concerned, however, to show why the erroneous positions have proved to be so tempting. One such factor may be briefly noted now. It may well be that those who prepared the recommendations on bilingualism and bi-culturalism were *in fact* open-minded people, not locked into traditional and often limited views of other cultures, ready to revise their assessments in the light of new evidence and changing circumstances. Here, however, the fact of their open-mindedness is established independently of any consideration of the specific recommendations made. It is established in terms of their disposition to revise their views rationally. But there is a very powerful temptation, once we learn what their specific views are, to think that they are open-minded *because* they have these views.

A further point should be noted. In arguing that it does not follow logically from holding a certain view that A is open-minded, I do not, nor do I intend to, prejudge the *empirical* question concerning the likelihood of certain recommenda-tions and proposals serving to *promote* an open-minded atti-tude among Canadians. This hope was indeed expressed in the *Report of the Royal Commission on Bilingualism and Bicultur-alism* when it referred to the possible breaking down of rigid attitudes, and it is an empirical question how far such hope has been or will be realised. It is itself a question about which one can be open- or closed-minded. I allow, therefore, that it may well be that something like A's position is in fact more likely to promote open-mindedness in Canada (with respect to certain issues) than B's position. But this is altogether different from, nor does it entail, the view that B's position is held in a closed-minded fashion.

With these qualifications in mind, it is time to turn now to a critical examination of the alternative views which I have claimed are false.

2/ Content as a necessary condition? Objections:

(a) If specific beliefs were a necessary condition of open-mindedness, then we would not be entitled to ascribe the trait if we did not know (or did not think we knew) the person's opinions. In the situation, however, in which a person has no specific opinion because he has not yet made up his mind, clearly we cannot know his opinion. Yet a person who is still trying to make up his mind on the basis of all available argument and evidence is properly said to be open-minded. If a specific opinion were demanded, then neutrality would be inconsistent with open-mindedness whereas it is, of course, commonly the case that one's very open-mindedness leads one to be neutral. This is not to say that neutrality is either necessary or sufficient for open-mindedness, but only that it is not inconsistent with it.

(b) If a specific belief were a necessary condition of open-mindedness, then the process of inquiry which first led to the discovery of that belief could not be characterized as open-minded. But we often want to characterize a process as open-minded before we know the results.

(c) Although we might find *as a matter of fact* that all those who accept a certain view have closed minds and that only those who reject such views are open-minded, these facts are discovered independently of the fact that those persons do or do not hold a certain view. We might find that only members of a certain group are in fact closed-minded, perhaps as the result of a highly efficient indoctrination program. Then we could say "Only those who hold this set of beliefs are closed-minded." But we need to remember that this is a contingent statement and not a statement of a conceptual truth. No doubt the existence of such contingent truths encourages the view that certain opinions are logically necessary conditions of open-mindedness, for we do not always sufficiently distinguish: (i) "Only those who hold this belief are (in fact) closed-minded" and (ii) "Only those who hold this belief are (on that account) closed-minded." The problem is compounded by the fact that sometimes we know on empirical grounds that a person does not come to hold a certain opinion unless subjected to intense indoctrination, i.e., that in our world indoctrination is a *causally* necessary condition of holding certain views. Then from the fact that he holds a certain view we can infer that he has been indoctrinated (using this for a process which leads to having a closed-mind). At this point, we are in danger of confusing causal and logical conditions and concluding that holding a certain view necessarily entails a closed-mind. In our earlier example, B may well be *prepared* to listen seriously to arguments against his position on the rights of minority linguistic groups and be prepared to abandon it if a good case can be made out against it. This is logically possible. The mere content of the opinion does not show that this is logically impossible, however unlikely it may be. This is because it is not inconsistent to say, for any belief p, "A believes p but is prepared to abandon it in the light of counter-evidence or argument," except where the belief is itself presupposed in the idea of open-mindedness as is the case with certain logical principles.[2]

(d) It might, however, be objected that content is ultimately necessary because if B in the case above *is* seriously listening to objections, he cannot fail to see that they destroy his position. Since, however, he persists in his belief, he cannot really be considering the counter-arguments of A. Thus, *at most*, the specific content criterion is *deferred* until the arguments have been considered. Then if B is open-minded, he will give up his position. In case it might appear that such objections are "straw-man" arguments, it is fortunate that a similar argument can be found in serious philosophy, in this instance in the writings of Descartes. One of Descartes' reasons for believing that in matters of ongoing controversy neither party to the dispute can properly be said to know the answer is that "If the reasoning of the second was sound and clear he would be able to lay it before the other as finally to succeed in convincing his understanding also."[3] Descartes here, and our imaginary objector above, assume that clear and sound reasoning will necessarily be recognized as such by all who seriously attend. But, of course, we want to reply to Descartes, quite apart from the fact that the man in his example may not be very *persuasive* (Descartes assumes that what one can understand one can necessarily teach), the listener may simply fail to see that the argument is valid. And, to return to our example, B may fail to see the merits in A's counter-arguments, and this failure does not show that he was not trying, or trying not, to see them, nor that he is pretending not to have seen them. As Aristotle ruefully noted, "Argument and teaching, it is to be feared, do not always have the same power."[4] Of course, B may be so simple- or feeble-minded that he cannot seriously attend to the arguments, but then it is not his failure to hold certain beliefs, but his inability to do certain things, which makes the concept of open-mindedness inapplicable to him.

(e) Finally, it might be urged that it is surely necessary that an open-minded person have at least this opinion, namely, that he is himself fallible and liable to be wrong. This may well be an instance of a contingently true statement of the kind discussed in (c) above, i.e., that there are no instances of open-minded persons who think they are infallible. But is this a logically necessary truth? The person who believes that he is infallible thinks that his opinion either will not, or could not, turn out to be mistaken. Such a person will, of course, think it *pointless* to examine his claims once made or to reconsider them, but he could do those things if only to show everyone that he is right. He might even be prepared to answer objections from those who argue that he cannot be infallible. Since such a person has the utmost confidence in his opinions, he would have no reason to fear the outcome of a serious and critical examination of them.

3/ Content as a Sufficient Condition?

(a) Indoctrination

It is surely an obvious objection, to the claim that A (in our earlier example of views on the language rights of minority groups) is necessarily open-minded because he has a certain view, that people can be indoctrinated into holding particular beliefs. Dictionaries commonly indicate that one aspect of open-mindedness is "not having rigidly fixed views" where the emphasis is on *rigidly*. (I will consider how this point may have been misunderstood when I examine the concept of neutrality shortly.) D. J. O'Connor captured this sense when he spoke of the open-minded person not making up his mind "finally and irrevocably."[5] He did not mean by this that something could not be a man's *last* opinion, one that he does not *in fact* reject or revoke. Clearly, good objections to our view may never arise in our lifetime. O'Connor is referring to a way of holding on to beliefs in defiance of what we see to be decisive counter-evidence. It is one thing to believe that a view is final and quite another to make up one's mind in the manner suggested by O'Connor. The former is compatible with being prepared to revise one's view, but the latter precisely excludes this. If a person says, "I will believe p whatever the future evidence may be," it is not his belief in p which makes him a person with a closed mind but his determination to hold on to p at all costs. However admirable A's opinion may be, it might be held in this dogmatic and inflexible way. A might refuse to listen to B's point of view. He might want B censored and punished. No particular belief in and of itself guarantees that the person holding it will be willing to revise it in the light of future evidence, nor that the person has come to hold it as a result of rationally considering the alternatives. Again we may well find many useful empirical generalizations here such as, for example, that people who hold such beliefs tend to be willing to revise them or that people who hold such beliefs tend to do so because they have rationally weighed the alternatives. But we must take care not to turn these empirical generalizations into conceptual claims. When we come (in chapter 6) to examine various procedures in teaching, such as discussion, considering, lecturing, listening, etc., we will see that there has been a great temptation to argue that the development of certain traits of intellect, such as open-mindedness, is ruled out *in principle* by the use of certain methods, when the claim should be stated as an empirical issue. Moreover, conceptual connections between, for example, discussion and open-mindedness have been turned into procedural principles, as if armchair or even office desk conceptual work could guarantee certain results by certain methods.

(b)   A counter-example?

It might be countered, however, that, granting the above is in general correct, there is at least one counter-example, namely, the case of the man who is of the opinion that any belief should be rejected if good counter-evidence is produced. To this, however, it might first be objected that this does not show that the person has been operating thus far in an open-minded manner, rationally considering alternatives. It may be that he does not even recognize revisability as a condition of rational inquiry, but has been induced irrationally to believe it. (I do not, of course, imply by this that if a person is induced irrationally to believe p, that he will (can) never come to think about p in an open-minded manner. I mean merely that the possibility of irrational conviction prevents us from inferring that his earlier inquiries *were* open-minded.) But secondly, the person's practice may well fall short of what we might expect of someone holding this opinion, even if it is sincerely held by someone who sees that it is a condition of rational inquiry. I am aware that there are limits to backsliding, so that certain behaviour might lead us to say that the person does not have the opinion at all. But short of this, failures could be sufficiently serious and numerous to make us say that although this is the man's opinion, his failure to live up to it warrants withholding the trait-ascription. We might say that he knows what open-mindedness is, he thinks he should be open-minded, but unfortunately he is not. I conclude then that specific beliefs are neither necessary nor sufficient conditions of open-mindedness and that *a fortiori* open-mindedness is not equivalent to believing certain things.

4/ The criterion of neutrality

It was argued in section 2 (above) that specific beliefs cannot be said to be demanded by open-mindedness because it may be that the individual has not yet made up his mind about the question. This, of course, was not meant to imply that one must be neutral in order to be open-minded; for with respect to some of his specific beliefs an individual can be said to be open-minded. If neutrality were a necessary condition, the expression "an open-minded Catholic" would contain a contradiction, but indeed one distinction we often want to make is between those religious persons who are open-minded and those who are not with respect to aspects of their religion. This condition would entail that, with respect to belief in God, only the agnostic can be open-minded and this is simply not how the concept operates in our thinking. Furthermore, since neutrality would be a foolish position to adopt with respect to all those issues which are properly regarded as *settled* (e.g., former disputes about the position of the earth in the universe), open-mindedness would come to be restricted to the area of ongoing controversy. This latter view has proved to be attractive even to those who do not link neutrality with open-mindedness. John Dewey, for example, in a section headed "Open-mindedness" wrote: "Openness of mind means accessibility of mind to any and every consideration that will throw light upon the situation that needs to be cleared up, and that will help determine the consequences of acting this way or that."[6] But the phrase "the situation that needs to be cleared up" places an arbitrary restriction on the scope of open-mindedness, for openness of mind is an important attitude to have to those situations which *are* cleared up, i.e., settled. We do expect that scientists will remain open-minded about matters of controversy, but we also expect them to remain open-minded about the best corroborated hypotheses, as, for example, Einstein did about his general theory of relativity.[7] The open-minded scientist remains ready to abandon his theory *if* counter-evidence begins to turn up. Philosophers of science like Popper argue that what serves to demarcate a scientific hypothesis is that it is in principle *falsifiable*. We can ask: Is the scientist prepared to accept that some things could in principle count against his hypothesis? In other words, is he being scientific? Thus, far from open-mindedness being ruled out because the scientist is non-neutral inasmuch as he has adopted certain hypotheses (or, as I shall say later, because he has *committed* himself), open-mindedness appears to be written into the notion of having a scientific outlook, inasmuch as this involves being willing to revise and/or reject the views one has in the light of fresh evidence.[8] This is not to say that everyone who is called a scientist, or who advances an hypothesis, actually has such an attitude. But if pseudo-scientific statements are such that nothing can ever count against them, then the *appropriate* attitude to have towards genuine scientific statements is that of open-mindedness because this recognizes the very vulnerability which is an essential mark of the scientific hypothesis. Certain English idioms are potentially misleading here, in particular, the phrase "an open question." We tend to use the latter with reference to issues which are as yet not settled. It is open in the sense that the resolution could go in more than one way. It is not difficult to imagine how the idea could develop that *open-mindedness* is an attitude only appropriate to open questions in this sense, and hence come to be restricted to matters of controversy. Rather open-mindedness recognizes that all questions remain open in the sense that there remains a permanent possibility of reopening even settled issues.

5/   Doubt as a necessary condition?

In view of these objections, another position is often adopted, one which essentially abandons neutrality but tries to make a last-ditch gesture in its direction. It is agreed that the open-minded person can have opinions, i.e., he need not be neutral, but he must not hold his opinions very firmly. Bertrand Russell, for example, although not wanting to equate open-mindedness and neutrality, said: "When you come to a point of view, maintain it with doubt. This doubt is precious because it suggests an open mind."[9] Admittedly this comment occurs not in a formal piece of philosophy but in correspondence, and may be interpreted as *pragmatic* advice, useful in view of the common tendency to accept beliefs uncritically. Furthermore, Russell does say only that it *suggests* an open mind and not that doubt is a necessary condition of an open mind. Still the view that open-mindedness excludes firm belief is common (perhaps because of the popular view that we cannot really know anything anyway, because knowledge is "subjective and relative"), and it is worth showing that it is false. Indeed, I have already argued above that particular beliefs cannot be stated as necessary conditions of open-mindedness, hence one cannot say that the belief that all our beliefs are uncertain is necessary. We need to distinguish a doubtful state of mind from the readiness to submit all claims to the test of evidence and argument. That a person submits his knowledge-claims to the court of rational inquiry does not mean that he *suspects* they are faulty. Let us consider an instance of a philosopher having no doubts about his beliefs and being willing to regard them as revisable. Hume had just observed that "where men are the most sure and arrogant, they are commonly the most mistaken," when he added: "Yet, I must confess, this enumeration puts the matter in so strong a light, that I cannot *at present* be more assured of any truth which I learn from reasoning and argument."[10] The italicized phrase is important, for Hume is making the point that he has no doubts *now*; but future events might bring him to see defects which he does not now see and cannot even imagine. He may come to doubt what he does not doubt now as a result of critical examination. (Or he may, after a period of doubts, come back to the *same* view having, as Descartes said in a fine example of open-mindedness, "adjusted them by the plumb-line of reason.")[11]

Suppose also that we accept Popper's view that scientific theories, if they are not falsified, forever remain hypotheses or conjectures.[12] They can never, that is, be established beyond the possibility of future revision. But I can acknowledge that a theory *could* be falsified while feeling quite sure that it is correct and being entitled to feel sure that it is correct. "Future evidence could go against it" does not imply "It is not certain." That it could turn out to be false does not imply that I feel uncertain about it, nor that I ought to feel uncertain about it. We can maintain well-corroborated hypotheses firmly,[13] without being accused of holding them rigidly. We will, if we are rational, have a firm preference for a theory which is well-corroborated over one which is less well-corroborated, but whether or not we are rigid, inflexible, or dogmatic thinkers depends upon our willingness to rethink our position if the theory suffers in an attempted refutation. If, however, our view is not simply that the theory is *liable* to be falsified, but is for some reason *likely* to be falsified, then if we are reasonable, our degree of confidence in it will be adjusted to our calculation of the likelihood. There could, however, clearly be situations in which there are some reasons for thinking that a view *may* be shown to be false, yet there are other, and stronger, grounds for thinking that it will not be. Thus even here a person's belief or confidence could be quite firm without any suggestion that he has closed his mind to the existence of the reasons which indicate that the view *may* be shown to be false. He should not, however, in these circumstances hold that the view is certain. I conclude then that the view that firm convictions rule out open-mindedness contributes to what Joel Feinberg has called "that corruption of the ideal of open-mindedness where everything is always 'up for grabs'."[14]

6/   Commitment incompatible with open-mindedness?

It is perhaps necessary, however, to introduce here some more detailed comments on the concept of commitment, for my preceding remarks may fail to convince those who are persuaded that there is something in the idea of being *committed* to a position which rules out open-mindedness. Thus, even if neutrality is not necessary, and a case may even be made for firm belief or preference, still, it may be argued, one cannot (logically) be committed to a position *and* remain open-minded about it. It is important to achieve clarity here because there are as many voices calling for commitment in education as for open-mindedness, and we need to know if these concepts are incompatible.[15] Do we have to choose between them?

(a) Logical commitment

Let us consider first the notion of logical commitment. If a conclusion *follows necessarily* from certain premises, then these premises *commit* one to the conclusion, i.e., we are committed *by* the premises *to* the conclusion. A person may not recognize that a certain conclusion follows necessarily, but he may be told "You are committed then to this." Now in this case, we have no reason to believe that he is not open-minded, for he may well be trying hard to see the point which others are insisting upon. He may, of course, never see this if he is simple-minded. But unless he is so lacking in intellectual ability that the ascription of a trait of intellect such as open-mindedness or closed-mindedness becomes inappropriate, his open-mindedness or lack of it is not decided by his *seeing* the point, but by his willingness to *look for* the point.

Consider secondly the case of the individual who recognizes that the acceptance of certain premises *commits* him to a certain conclusion. Is there room for open-mindedness here? Surely there is, in at least two ways:

(i) The person may continue to subject the premises to ongoing critical scrutiny and be willing to reject or revise them, depending upon how they stand up to tests.

(ii) The person may continue to entertain objections to his view that the conclusion follows necessarily, i.e., to his view that these premises *do* commit him to this conclusion. His present view that they do certainly commit him does not mean that he feels, or ought to feel, that this view could not be shown to be erroneous. (We know that many arguments held to be valid have later been shown not to be so.)

(b)   Rational commitment

The notion of commitment has an important role to play in discussions of controversial matters. Consider, for example, the contemporary debates over the alleged significance of Vitamin C in inhibiting the onset of the common cold, or the alleged significance of genetic factors on intellectual development. Neither of these issues could (at the present time) be said to be *settled* — they are conjectures which require much more by way of attempted refutations, and we do not know now if they will stand or fall. There is conflicting evidence and crucial tests have not yet been made. Still these positions have their champions, notably in the case of the former, Linus Pauling, and in the latter, Arthur Jensen. These men hold that, although many reasonable and intelligent men remain unconvinced of the truth of their hypotheses, the weight of the evidence tends to support them and that this evidence *commits* them to the position that they subscribe to. They have taken a stand on a controversial topic because they believe that the available evidence *forces* them to that view. Although it is not a matter of logical commitment as in the earlier case where a conclusion *follows necessarily*, still it is a matter of being swayed by reasons and evidence, and hence I dub this *rational commitment* — the adoption of the position is not merely arbitrary.[16] The negative form of this is very common in ordinary talk for if I want to *deny* that I took a stand, or made a recommendation, I may say that I did not *commit* myself. In logical commitment, the idea of being bound, obliged, or forced is present (e.g., I'm bound to accept this because I have accepted that) and this occurs too with rational commitment for the person feels bound to accept a certain conclusion in the light of the evidence. And when I do not commit myself, I refuse to involve myself with, or bind myself to, something by an expression of opinion or intention. Pauling and Jensen *have* committed themselves, i.e., they have associated themselves with certain theses by expressing certain opinions in their writings and this commitment is rationally based because it rests on evidence and argument.

The fact that the person is bound in various ways (logically, morally, legally, etc.) means that there are various challenges which may properly be put to him in certain circumstances which he will have to answer. It is thus that the concept often features in situations in which a person has to defend himself in some way, e.g., against the charge that something absurd follows from his position, or the charge that he has failed to keep his word, or the charge that the evidence does not warrant the conclusion he has drawn. Thus, although it is true that all the evidence *does* commit us to the view that George Eliot is the author of *Middlemarch*, we would not ordinarily *say* that we are committed to the view that George Eliot is the author of *Middlemarch* since no one seriously doubts this and hence we are not going to have to defend it. We would misleadingly convey an atmosphere of controversy were we to say that we were committed to this view rather than if we said quite simply that we know that she is the author. Consider how different is the case of the authorship of the *Seventh Letter*, where scholars do not agree that it should be attributed to Plato. Here a person might naturally say that he was committed to the view that Plato is the author, because he is satisfied that the weight of the evidence supports that view. He recognizes, however, that controversy persists, and he must be prepared to defend his view. It does not imply that he has himself any doubts about the authorship.

From the fact that a scholar is prepared to defend a controversial view, we cannot infer that he is not prepared to abandon it in any circumstances. He is prepared to defend it *now* because he subscribes to it, and he may also be prepared to reject it when he is shown the flaws in it. We cannot know *a priori* that a debate between two scholars who take different views on a controversial topic must be devoid of the open-minded spirit. Surely the only way to discover whether or not Russell and Copleston were closed-minded in their famous debate on the existence of God is to examine what they had to say, and how they reacted to what the other had to say.[17] There is no reason in principle why a person could not be both rationally committed to X and open-minded about it. This kind of commitment does not necessarily imply inflexibility, an unwillingness to abandon one's view in the face of a clear refutation or a good reason not to follow a proposed course of action. Fowler's *Dictionary of Modern English Usage* points out that, particularly in literary criticism, the word "committed" has come to be applied to those critics who are *fanatical* champions of a particular school, or those who have "blind obsessions." In this area, it has in short become a term of abuse, and a synonym for "dogmatic" and "prejudiced." Of course, if we use commitment *in this way*, it becomes *by definition* incompatible with open-mindedness. And since conceptual revision does occur, it could conceivably happen that "committed" might come to have this meaning in all contexts. This is, however, not now the case. But even if this were to happen, the important point for the concept of open-mindedness would be that this redefinition does not alter the substantive point that a scholar like Linus Pauling can be absolutely convinced that his view is correct *and* be open-minded about it. If this kind of redefinition occurred, we might want to deny that a particular scholar was "committed" in this new sense.

"Committed" has also come to have the sense of dedicated, no doubt because a dedicated person is one who takes his obligations, pledges, ties, commitments, responsibilities, ideals, etc., seriously and tries to honour them. (Similarly, we find phrases such as "a sense of responsibility" or "a responsible individual.") Recently, there have been some instances where "dedicated" has been used to suggest a blind, fanatical, unthinking allegiance.[18] Thus, by association, being committed may be taken to involve a closed mind. Again certain fanatical movements *demand* blind allegiance from their members, and A will be said to be not "really" committed if he pauses to look at the views of the opposition. But this is an attempt to arbitrarily redefine a desirable attitude into something quite different and undesirable by insisting that this new and different attitude is actually the genuine or true form, the other being only a deceptive fake. The move is often successful, unfortunately, because it takes over all the desirable associations of the former attitude by using the same term, and apparently making the mild suggestion that the proposed attitude is simply the true form. Or it may appear to be suggesting higher standards of the same attitude for its members because it rules out activities they might find interesting (such as listening to the views of others) and this serves to disguise the fact that it is attempting to replace one attitude, namely open-mindedness, with another, namely dogmatism.

(c) Ultimate commitment
It does not follow, however, that if a person is committed to a proposition or a procedure for which good reasons can in principle be given (by someone) that the person in question has a rational commitment. We can also bind ourselves by oaths, pledges, etc., to positions for which *we* have no rational defence. A person can say, "I believe in God," and have this as a firm belief though he can provide no rational foundation for the belief. The notion of commitment is very commonly employed in language to suggest a matter of faith, dogma, or basic conviction or allegiance which cannot be given further, or indeed any, rational support, either in principle or by the person who holds it. People often say, "This is where I take a stand—it's a matter of commitment." Consider a belief in an after-life. For some, this is no doubt a rational commitment, for they believe that there are some grounds for believing that such a state will come about. (Some might even claim to *know* this.) For many, however, it is simply something they believe in (let us call this an *ultimate* commitment); they could not give any defence of their view, but they believe it nonetheless: "I just think there will be an after-life, that's all." We would never say, "I just *consider* there will be an after-life, that's all."

If a person is not willing to consider objections to his ultimate commitment, then clearly he does not hold it in an open-minded way. But it may be asked: does it make any sense to talk of being open-minded with respect to one's ultimate commitments? I think the following case is possible. A person believes in an after-life, though he does not think that there are any good reasons for this belief, and similarly, feels that the arguments against such a belief are equally inconclusive. Perhaps the person believes that argument can never settle this issue and that indeed such issues are in principle outside the realm of rational resolution. Still, it is not inconceivable that this individual could continue to listen seriously to those who think the issue *can* be resolved, and be prepared to give up his belief if a case against belief in an after-life is made out to his satisfaction. He holds it without rational support, i.e., it is an ultimate commitment by definition, but the possibility of rational rejection is not excluded. Conversely, he may be prepared to turn his ultimate commitment into a rational commitment in the event that a good case for a belief in an after-life appears.

I only claim, of course, that the above makes *sense*, not that it is at all common. Often people explain away instances which conflict with their ultimate commitments. For example, a person is held to be infallible. Nothing is going to be allowed to falsify this. If something appears to do so, then it is only an apparent inconsistency. The infallible statement will be reinterpreted to accommodate the instance, or it will be denied that it was ever made, and so on.

It is necessary at this point to consider the objection that rational commitment itself collapses into ultimate commitment of the closed-minded variety, for while a person is prepared to give reasons for his views and listen to the reasons others have, he is wedded to the principle of reason-giving — for him, this is an ultimate commitment, and he has a closed-mind on it. Nothing will persuade him to abandon it.

In reply, we need to insist that a person cannot give a reason for the principle of reason-giving without *presupposing* the practice he is allegedly defending.[19] Whereas in the case of commitments to religious and political positions, it always makes sense at least to ask for a person's reasons, this is not the case with the principle of reason-giving itself. It is logically impossible to ask for a reason here without at the same time invoking the principle in question. It is not then appropriate to level the charge of irrationality here, for this charge surely applies in a context in which reasons *might* be given but are not, or one in which we fly in the face of good reason. In the case of reason-giving itself, no reason can be given in any way which does not beg the issue. Thus it is misleading to characterize this in terms which suggest that a potentially open inquiry is somehow arbitrarily closed off.[20] We rightly object to ultimate commitment when it jeopardizes the pursuit of truth, but this objection cannot apply to the principle of reason-giving, for our concepts of truth and rationality are linked, though not, of course, identical. We are justified in thinking that p is true when some evidence, argument, reason, establishes it.

There is no contradiction, despite an air of paradox, in the idea of a person being committed to open-mindedness. The sense of a contradiction is generated when we think of commitment as suggesting a fanatical, inflexible, irrational stance. But this difficulty is apparent rather than real. To be committed to open-mindedness is just to have a well-established disposition to think open-mindedly and not to be prone to fall short of the standards built into this ideal. It is freely adopted by the person as a requirement of rationality. One cannot be open-minded about one's open-mindedness (except insofar as one may accept temporary restraints in extraordinary circumstances on open-mindedness), but this is simply because any attempt at open-mindedness here will of necessity presuppose that attitude. But where relevant reasons against one's view cannot in principle arise, one cannot be accused of arbitrarily ignoring them.

(d) Moral commitment

We might finally consider our moral commitments. To say, in this sense, that one has a commitment, or has made a commitment, is to say that one has engaged oneself to do something, that one is involved in a promise or an undertaking. A person's moral commitment is normally either his agreeing to do something or what it is he has agreed to do.[21] We can also have commitments which derive from the law as when we have a commitment tomorrow morning (for jury service). These fall on us: we do not initiate them. Clearly, open-mindedness here does not involve searching around for reasons which would show that we should not keep our promises or should not turn up at the law court. But the open-minded person will not treat these as *absolute*, for some consideration might show that the commitment should not be honoured, i.e., if some consideration overrides the commitment.

7/ Neutrality as a sufficient condition?

It might still be maintained that though one need not be neutral in order to be open-minded, still if one *is* neutral then one is open-minded. This view gains support in part from what Hume called "the caprice of language."[22] We have the expression "to keep an open-mind on the matter." For example, J. P. Corbett, discussing ideological neutrality and the liberal university, comments: "Officially, liberal society keeps an open mind towards such rivals as Catholicism and Marxism."[23] Neutrality is a sufficient condition of having an open mind in this sense—indeed it is equivalent to it. It is not difficult to imagine how the existence of this expression could have generated the popular view that *open-mindedness* also demands that a person may not have made up his mind, or that not having made up your mind shows that you are open-minded. This false view gains further support from the fact that the statement "I've made up my mind" is sometimes employed with that finality which suggests a closed mind. These connotations, however, should not lead us to believe that open-mindedness is the same as neutrality of opinion or even that it is implied by neutrality. We have already seen how a person can be open-minded without being neutral, hence they cannot be the same. It only remains to show conversely how a person could be neutral without being open-minded.

A person may remain neutral, i.e., in the state of not having made up his mind, about some issue, because he cannot be bothered to think seriously about the dispute or does not want to get or be involved. He is familiar with the issue, understands what is involved, but has not pursued the matter. Asked where he stood on the controversy, he might well say he was neutral. This would not show that he was open-minded, nor indeed would it show that he had a closed mind. With respect to this issue, these terms do not seem to apply at all. It is only in terms of a person's reactions to the evidence and argument when he begins to consider the issue that such assessments will begin to apply. *A fortiori* his neutrality in this case can do nothing to establish the more general claim that he is an open-minded person.

The case is quite different if an individual reserves judgment on an issue because, having considered all the available evidence and argument, he cannot decide which side is in the right. Here the individual is neutral *and* open-minded, but it is not his neutrality *per se* which guarantees his open-mindedness. The latter follows when we discover that he is maintaining a neutral position until some reason is presented which obliges him to take a stand on the issue.

8/ Ignorance as a sign of open-mindedness?

Though strictly speaking ignorance does not fall under neutrality, since we only call people neutral if they have *some* familiarity with the issue in question, it is convenient to consider it here as a possible criterion of open-mindedness inasmuch as it shares with neutrality the feature of not being committed. It follows from our earlier arguments that ignorance cannot be a requirement of open-mindedness, since we have shown how A can be open-minded about what he knows. Is there any reason to think that ignorance ensures open-mindedness? Some philosophers have attempted to establish a link. Thus John Dewey wrote: "Genuine ignorance is more profitable because it is likely to be accompanied by humility, curiosity and open-mindedness, while ability to repeat catch phrases, cant terms, familiar propositions gives the conceit of learning and coats the mind with a varnish waterproof to new ideas."[24] It is possible that a similar idea lies behind Descartes' claim that "those who have learned the least of all that has hitherto been called philosophy are the most capable of learning the true one."[25] The idea which is at work in both of these cases may be that found in Plato's observation that a person is not likely to look for, or attempt to learn, what he thinks he already knows.[26] The conceit of learning referred to by Dewey (an echo of Plato's criticism of the Sophists) is that of believing we know something when we do not. And Descartes is referring to those who have acquired the false opinions of traditional philosophy which have "prejudiced their minds." The suggestion is that the person who has learned nothing of these matters will be more accessible to new ideas than the person who has acquired either pieces of information without understanding, or false beliefs.

None of these claims is acceptable if understood as a conceptual claim. They must all be taken as psychological generalizations, even though they are propounded by those who are known chiefly as philosophers. To consider Plato's view first, we can point out that there is no reason *in principle* why a person who thinks he knows could not continue to examine the belief he holds. Similarly, it can be replied to Descartes that it is perfectly possible to replace a false belief with a true one. (Indeed there are many cases where it will be extremely difficult to *understand* the true belief unless one has worked one's way through erroneous positions. The study of philosophy itself provides examples of this, when an understanding of previous positions taken is very important to our grasp of contemporary positions which have superseded them.[27] The man who is ignorant of the historical positions may be willing to receive new ideas but unable to do so.) There is nothing in the possession of a false belief *per se* which hinders the grasp of the true position, though it is certainly the case that certain ways of holding the belief (dogmatically, arrogantly, with finality, etc.) can be a hindrance. In considering Dewey's suggestion we need to distinguish the person who is ignorant of the theory, issue, matter, view, etc., and the person who is ignorant of the answer, resolution, true belief, etc. In the first case, the concept of open- or closed-mindedness seems not to apply at all, for the person must have some familiarity with whatever he is said to be open- or closed-minded about. Newton may have been open-minded about his own theory, but it is nonsense to claim that he was open-minded about the (then unknown) theory of relativity. This is a reason, I believe, for treating with caution Dewey's further suggestion that "open-mindedness means retention of the childlike attitude."[28] Very young children do not as yet have minds which are made up "finally and irrevocably" and in early years typically demonstrate a willingness to learn new things. But while it is true that they do not have closed minds, we cannot say that they are open-minded with respect to matters of which they are entirely ignorant. I am not sure that open-mindedness applies to them at all until they begin to realize that beliefs can be revised, that one can get locked into beliefs, and that it is important to examine fresh evidence.[29]

In the second case, i.e., of the individual who is ignorant of the answer, solution, etc., there is no *necessary* connection between ignorance and open-mindedness. There is no contradiction at all in saying that someone did not know x, and yet refused to consider it as a possible answer when it was proposed. Apparently it had not occurred to Queen Victoria that there might be such a thing as a lesbian relationship. But her genuine ignorance here did not prevent her from refusing to believe that such a practice might exist. We cannot say *a priori* that the person who is genuinely ignorant of x will be more willing to entertain some thesis about x than the person who has some beliefs about x, even when these beliefs conflict with the thesis proposed. In brief, each of these claims at best assert a contingent truth, i.e., they tell us something about the circumstances in which open-mindedness *in fact* occurs. They do not tell us anything about the logic of the concept.

9/ Conclusion

We cannot tell then from knowledge of a person's beliefs, or from knowledge of his neutrality or non-neutrality, or from evidence of his ignorance or doubts, whether or not he is open-minded. And our knowledge that a person is open-minded does not tell us what his beliefs are or whether or not he is neutral with respect to some issue, though it does tell us that he is at least familiar with that issue he is said to be open-minded about. Whatever his particular beliefs, and whether or not he is neutral, and despite his knowledge of a solution or lack of knowledge, the open-minded person is one who is willing to look seriously at new evidence, theories, and arguments, and ready to base his beliefs and decisions on the best assessment he can make of these. Thus when we read that Plotinus said, "But if when Porphyry asks questions we do not solve his difficulties, we shall not be able to say anything at all to put into the treatise,"[30] we detect the attitude of an open-minded philosopher, though we may know nothing of his philosophical beliefs.

Examples of the closed-mind are not hard to find. In the *Montreal Star*, June 3, 1976, there appeared a letter, written by one who claimed to represent the Montreal Committee Against Racism, which referred to a lecture which Hans Eysenck had given at McGill University. The writer said:

> However, the goal of our protest was for people to boycott the lecture. We leafletted extensiyely and the fact that not more than 125 people showed up at the 350 capacity hall indicates the success of the protest. If ... there were no blacks in our picket, there were also none listening to Mr. Eysenck because the black communities decided to ignore him completely, a further measure of success. ... His speech was certainly not bland. It made the usual unfounded claim that personality and intelligence were mainly based on genetic inheritance.

We are clearly a long way here from being unwilling to make claims before we have answered our opponents' "difficulties," to echo Plotinus. This writer measures "success" by the extent to which an opponent is *ignored*. People are urged not to listen to certain views, but are then expected apparently to accept a potted (and, no doubt, distorted) account written by someone else. Without doubt, many people who are opposed to racism *are* open-minded, but this person is not one of them and his misguided zeal and sense of mission do not obscure the fact that he has a closed mind.[31]

Other powerful emotions, such as fear, can have the same inhibiting effect on open inquiry. A good example is the controversy surrounding alleged wonder drugs in the treatment of cancer. Canada has had its own home-grown remedy in Essiac, but by far the greatest furor has been in the United States in connection with an extract from apricot pits, Laetrile. Now the belief in the medical establishment that Laetrile is ineffective, typified by the Harvard neurosurgeon who pronounced the drug "pure quackery," is not in itself closed-minded. We need to know how the belief is arrived at, and the holder's disposition to review the evidence and/or to test the claims. Even here we need to be careful, for a reluctance even to *undertake* a clinical test might reflect a belief that such a *test*, quite apart from any outcome, might mislead the public. Similarly, those who support Laetrile may or may not be open-minded. If, for example, Dr. Robert Eyerley (*Newsweek*, June 27, 1977) were right that such people would remain convinced no matter how ineffective the tests showed Laetrile to be, then these people would be closed-minded, for they would not be willing to revise or reject a belief in the light of counter-evidence.

Open-mindedness and education

3

1/ Preliminary comments

We are now in a position to turn to some important issues in the philosophy of education.

(a) Is the concept of open-mindedness connected with the concept of education? Is it a necessary or a sufficient condition of being educated? Does open-mindedness exclude other attitudes which might be thought to be of value?

(b) What would it mean for a person to be an open-minded teacher? If open-mindedness is not the same as neutrality or impartiality, could it yet be that open-minded teaching demands neutrality on the part of the teacher? Do certain general teaching strategies, such as formal instruction, necessarily clash with open-minded teaching? And do others, such as discussion, guarantee open-minded teaching?

(c) Are there any good reasons for the view that certain issues, in particular controversial issues, should not even be *considered* in schools? Can a good case against open-mindedness in schools be made? Let us turn immediately to the first of these groups of questions for our interest in methods of teaching is subordinate to our interest in the aims of education.

2/   A Logical Difficulty?

It was noted in chapter 1 that the term "open-mindedness" carries with it generally favourable overtones. It is, in short, typically viewed as a desirable intellectual virtue. This is not, however, universally the case, and such a distinguished critic of education as Jacques Barzun refers to it as "one degree worse than a sieve."[1] This may, of course, reflect a different understanding of the term, perhaps a confusion with a vacant or empty mind, but still it reminds us of the need to show in what way the trait is, according to the analysis provided, a virtue.

Prior to this, however, we need to consider a problem (which will crop up again when we look at open-mindedness in the context of teaching certain subjects), namely, the view that open-mindedness is not *possible*. Allport, for example, in his very influential work on prejudice, dismisses the claim that open-mindedness is a virtue because "strictly speaking, it cannot occur."[2] (It would be interesting, from an historical point of view, to investigate how far such a view accounts for the comparative lack of interest shown by educational theorists in the notion of open-mindedness compared, say, with the idea of neutrality.) What is Allport's reason for this view? He argues thus: "A new experience *must* be redacted into old categories. We cannot handle each event freshly in its own right. If we did so, of what use would past experience be?"[3] Notice that, although Allport is writing as a social psychologist, this comment does not read as an empirical claim. We saw in chapter 1 that Kohlberg claims to have found *empirical* evidence showing that the traditional virtues are mythical.[4] In the objection raised by Allport, however, it sounds as if he thinks he has found a reason why *in principle* open-mindedness is impossible. And this, it seems, is because new experiences must be interpreted by means of an existing conceptual framework—the old categories. We can readily agree, of course, that it is not at all easy to be open-minded, and that even if we achieve this attitude in some aspects of our thinking, there may be other areas in which our minds are closed. It is harder still to achieve a predominantly open-minded atmosphere in society as a whole. All this is confirmed by historians of thought[5] and social psychologists,[6] as well as in our own everyday experience. None of this evidence, however, shows that open-mindedness is logically beyond our reach, that it can no more exist than a square circle. It is important then to face up to Allport's challenge, because if open-mindedness logically cannot be attained, then we cannot work towards it and there is no point in recommending it. If, on the other hand, it is just extremely difficult to attain it, we can still hold on to it as an ideal, seek ways of removing the obstacles to it, and attempt to approach it more closely.

It may be admitted, in response to Allport, that we do try to make sense of a new experience in terms of the conceptual and theoretical framework which we possess. This does not mean, however, that all new experiences must be forced into a pre-existing mould which is sacrosanct. Even if new experiences were to be dealt with in terms of existing categories, open-mindedness is possible because it is open into *which* categories the experience is to be fitted. At times, however, there is no ready way to handle new experiences in terms of present concepts and theories, and we are forced to develop new categories, or even to modify and discard former ones. Let us consider some examples.

(a) Programmatic revision in art criticism

Before the work of innovative artists such as Marcel Duchamp, art critics worked with fairly sharp divisions between the categories of art objects, natural objects, and functional objects. In 1914 Duchamp purchased a bottle rack in a Paris store, signed it and had it displayed *as an art object* and challenged at once the adequacy of the existing divisions among categories. The concept of art has in the course of time been revised and modified to accommodate, for example, *objets trouvés*, and other developments introduced by creative artists. The new creations have been judged to be sufficiently similar to the already accepted class of art objects to warrant including them within a revised concept of art. There is perhaps no compelling reason to accept such revisions, and the traditionalist who wishes to maintain the earlier concept cannot be shown to be simply wrong or illogical. And yet the revision is by no means an arbitrary one. Here, as elsewhere in certain areas of philosophy, it is perhaps inappropriate, as Joel Feinberg has put it, to set about looking for "proofs" and "refutations."[7] Still, there are *points* which can be made in favour of enlarging the concept of art to include "found objects," such as that someone has called attention to the features of a natural or functional object which might otherwise have gone unnoticed, and has actually displayed the object so that those features could be looked at, enjoyed, and appreciated. These points make a difference, and ease the transfer from talk of a natural object to talk of an art object. Scheffler's comments on definitions in the area of art are apposite here:

> definitions of artistic innovators often extend the use of the term "work of art" to new sorts of objects; the counter definitions of conservatives withhold the term from these same objects. Both sets of definitions are, furthermore, often consonant with artistic tradition, that is, they are in conformity with prior usage. The dispute can thus not be taken, in such cases, to be a matter of the meanings of the terms alone. Rather, it is a question of divergent artistic programs, conveyed by opposing programmatic definitions that are also descriptively accurate.[8]

As Scheffler has made clear, the practical question we are faced with in such a case is whether or not X *ought* to be accorded the treatment normally given to the sorts of work previously called "works of art."[9] This is the sort of question to which we may bring arguments and counter-arguments, as I have already indicated. Conceptual revision here need not be arbitrary. Various sorts of consideration can be introduced in order to attempt a rational appraisal of the proposed revision. It is one thing to admit, as we may, that such considerations are notoriously controversial, but quite another to claim, what is false, that we are of necessity locked into the categories we presently possess beyond all possibility of rational reconsideration.

(b) Revision in philosophy

It is, of course, primarily art *critics* who, in such a case as the one above, propose to change the concept of "work of art," which they employ in their activity of criticism, in order to cope with the new situation. It is not the philosopher *qua philosopher* who makes such a change. But open-mindedness is possible too for the philosopher of art, for he may wish, or be obliged, to revise a theory he has about the nature of a concept such as "work of art." A theory about the conceptual relationship between "work of art" and "intention" might need to be modified in the light of changes in the use of the concept introduced by art critics. The philosopher's task is to examine the nature of the concepts we employ in talking about the world, and to criticize the theories of other philosophers about the nature of these concepts. Thus we continue to talk of "the mind" and employ mental concepts much as our ancestors did. Yet it is only partly true that the old categories persist. For our view of the *nature* of these categories has greatly altered as the result of philosophical argument. We continue to be open-minded in philosophy to the extent that we remain disposed to revise the theories we presently hold with respect to the nature of our concepts. *Philosophical* concepts, such as sense-data, material object, prescriptivity, etc., which are developed in order to describe and account for the logical behaviour of other concepts, may be revised or abandoned in the light of future philosophical argument.[10] That this can also be done rationally I tried to illustrate in chapter 2, by showing that alternative views about the concept of open-mindedness lead to incoherence or fail to account for acknowledged uses of the concept. Again, we are not irrevocably locked into our conception of a particular concept. We may begin by asking which specific beliefs a person must not hold if he or she is to be open-minded, and conclude, as we did in chapter 2, that the very *question* contains a mistake.

(c)   Revision of concepts and theories in science

There is a great deal of discussion in current epistemology and philosophy of science concerning the possibility of rational revision of scientific theories, paradigms, concepts, and categories, and it will not be possible, nor would it be appropriate, in this context to enter into the details of this complex controversy.[11] In chapter 5 I do discuss, and find reason to reject, a number of popular and influential arguments which attempt to show that the rational formation and revision of theories and claims in social science is impossible. I will not anticipate these arguments here, nor the more general relativistic attack from radical sociologists which is also examined in detail there.

We may, of course, freely admit that the *discovery* of new concepts and categories sometimes results from conjecture, intuition, chance, and an educated guess. Of course, the person who is not familiar with science is not at all likely to make an original suggestion, and thus there is much we can do to put ourselves in the situation where such discoveries may occur.[12] Still, there are no established *rules* or *methods* for producing original ideas, and unlike earlier philosophers we do not expect to find any such. We can accept, however, that the process of scientific discovery is not governed by rational rules of inference, without committing ourselves to the view that rational revision of scientific concepts is ruled out. The "discoveries" are initially put forward as *suggestions*, i.e., hypotheses, and the acceptance or rejection of such suggestions *is* subject to rational evaluation. As Carl Hempel puts it, "scientific objectivity is safeguarded by the principle that while hypotheses and theories may be freely invented and *proposed* in science, they can be *accepted* into the body of scientific knowledge only if they pass critical scrutiny, which includes in particular the checking of suitable test implications by careful observation or experiment."[13]

This point has an important application in the philosophy of education which is not generally recognized. Modern educators place a high value on permitting and encouraging the student to do original and creative work, and to discover ideas for himself.[14] This *can* be an important mark of an open-minded approach, for it recognizes that the student may come up with ideas, suggestions, and contributions which may lead to a reconsideration of our existing views. But insufficient attention has been paid to the fact that a genuine concern for open-mindedness carries with it the further requirement that the student's work itself be evaluated and assessed. Open-mindedness is not empty-mindedness; we are concerned to revise and reconsider, because we are concerned to get at the truth. If we encourage "creativity" and "discovery learning" in the name of open-mindedness, we must be concerned to go on to ask if the student *is* indeed getting at the truth. There is no reason to believe *a priori* that he must be. Proposals may be useful or useless, clear or confused. Far from it being the case that open-mindedness in teaching implies the view that "one opinion is as good as another," once the latter notion is operative open-mindedness is lost, for we have at this point abandoned the ideal of replacing our present views with better ones.

Allport fallaciously moves from the fact that we *come to* new experiences with a certain set of categories to the conclusion that the new experience must be *fitted into* that set of categories. Open-mindedness is possible just because we are aware that our existing conceptual and theoretical framework may not be adequate to deal with future experiences. Even if it were adequate, it itself consists of various alternatives which would have to be considered. Allport's mistake is reflected in the popular view that all teaching is necessarily indoctrinatory, because it involves passing on a certain framework to children. Even at the earliest stages of language acquisition, a conceptual orientation to the world is being acquired. Surely the response to this is that the very framework we possess can be used in order to bring us to a new position in which the old framework is modified or abandoned. This is what Einstein did with the Newtonian framework, what Picasso did with the prevailing artistic norms, and indeed what most of us do to a greater or lesser extent with the absolute moral rules we are taught as children. Since some creative thinkers have destroyed the framework which they grew up with, it cannot be impossible to produce a new framework for new experiences. And, as I have illustrated, the revision need not be an arbitrary one, something which *just happens*. Although it is *possible* to get locked into a particular framework, as successful indoctrination programs have shown, our concepts need not form a mental prison for us, but can provide a stepping-stone to new and hitherto undreamed-of ways of looking at the world. Educators sometimes talk as if teaching were somehow at odds with the child's creative development. Apart from the logical point that one *can* create new ideas from the basis of an existing framework which one has not created for oneself, all the empirical evidence would indicate that creative moves are only made by those who are well versed in the best existing theory or practice. In philosophy we have the examples of Kant who confessed to being awakened from a dogmatic slumber by Hume's work; and that of G. E. Moore who thought that philosophical problems would not have occurred to him had it not been for things which other philosophers had said. It is true, of course, as Descartes points out,[15] that many disciples of a great philosopher never get beyond that philosopher's framework. But as Descartes himself notes elsewhere,[16] it is not the study of the ideas of others *per se* which is the problem, but the attitude which we bring to that study. Open-mindedness does not, of course, mean that we refuse to apply an old category to a new experience, but that we are willing to consider in an open way which category best accommodates the new experience. Often an existing category is perfectly adequate and therefore useful. Even when the old category is finally abandoned, it may well have been useful inasmuch as without it the new insight would never have been achieved. It is not clear, for example, that we would have arrived at such clarification as we possess of mental concepts were it not for the pioneering "category mistakes" of the historical philosophers.[17] Open-mindedness then involves being willing to revise our existing categories if they are found to be inadequate in the light of new experiences.

3/ The principle of tenacity

Curiously, Allport does report the existence of what he calls "the somewhat rare condition of habitual open-mindedness."[18] "There are," he observes, "people who seem to go through life with little of the rubricizing tendency. ... Realising the complexity and variety in human nature, they are especially chary of ethnic generalizations. If they hold to any at all it is in a highly tentative way, and every contrary experience is allowed to modify the pre-existing ethnic concept."[19] Leaving aside the question of whether or not this can be reconciled with his own earlier statement, this assertion clearly suggests that open-mindedness may conflict with other valuable attitudes, such as a determination to persist with certain hypotheses or lines of inquiry until they are shown to be erroneous or become exhausted.

Notice that Allport is not saying that people who have been independently identified as open-minded tend to have the above characteristics. Rather he calls someone open-minded *because* he has such characteristics, i.e., these are, for him, defining characteristics of the state. We have already seen, in our earlier discussion of commitment, that open-mindedness does not rule out having firm beliefs. Our beliefs need not be held tentatively if this implies that we have little confidence in them. This is not to deny, of course, that with respect to certain generalizations (such as the ones referred to by Allport) empirical tests might show that all open-minded people do treat them with considerable suspicion. But we cannot logically infer from the fact that a person has great confidence in a particular ethnic generalization that the person has a closed mind.

It is also desirable that we do not give up our beliefs too readily, for we want to make sure *that* they are faulty, *why* they are faulty, and to rescue whatever element of truth there may be in them. It is important then to recognize that open-mindedness does not clash with this "principle of tenacity," as Basil Mitchell has dubbed it:

> Characteristically, the central postulates of the system are protected from alteration as long as possible and modifications are made at the periphery; and the impression is thus created that no counter-arguments will ever be allowed to count against the fundamental assertions of the system. This tendency is not unreasonable, for unless some "principle of tenacity" is accepted, the system will not be persevered with long enough for its potentialities to be thoroughly explored and tested.[20]

We might employ here a distinction drawn by Bryan Magee, who applied it to Karl Popper, and say that the open-minded person should be a naïve falsificationist at the level of logic but a highly critical falsificationist at the level of methodology.[21] It is clearly all too easy in practice to dismiss a person as being closed-minded just because he is anxious not to abandon his ground before he sees quite clearly why it should be abandoned. There are great demands on a teacher at this point, for he must not only insist that sound reasons be given to him before he gives up a position, but he must avoid creating the impression that nothing will make him give it up. In trying to see what is of value in a theory, we may decide at times to postpone consideration of objections and criticisms. But this temporary move need not suggest that we are closed-minded about the theory.

It is perhaps appropriate to discuss briefly in this context the connection between *ad hoc* hypotheses in science and open-mindedness. The phrase "*ad hoc* hypothesis" tends to be used pejoratively in scientific discussions to refer to an hypothesis which is introduced precisely and only to save some other favoured hypothesis from being refuted when contrary evidence derived from tests has emerged. We do, of course, sometimes judge hypotheses to be *ad hoc* suggestions, though we need to remember that, understood in the above way, this involves a judgment about the motivation of the person who introduces the hypothesis. And as Hempel reminds us, "with the benefit of hindsight, it seems easy to dismiss certain scientific suggestions of the past as *ad hoc* hypotheses."[22] With this caution in mind about the practical difficulties involved in detecting the *ad hoc* hypothesis, we can nevertheless draw a connection between *ad hoc* hypotheses and open-mindedness. If a scientist is to be open-minded, he must not produce merely *ad hoc* hypotheses, for by definition these are designed to protect some other hypothesis from being falsified, and producing them reveals the scientist's determination to hold on to his beliefs at all costs.

It is not, however, for every introduction of an additional or auxiliary hypothesis, when some other hypothesis appears to be threatened by test results, that a scientist is to be accused of closed-mindedness. When a predicted test implication, supposed to be derived from a certain scientific hypothesis in conjunction with one or more auxiliary hypotheses, is found not to occur, then it follows that the original hypothesis and the auxiliary hypothesis cannot *both* be true. But it may be the *auxiliary* hypothesis which is erroneous, and the introduction of a new auxiliary hypothesis may show that the original and main hypothesis is secure. It is here that we see the importance of Mitchell's principle of tenacity. The open-minded scientist remains ready to abandon his favoured hypothesis, but not until he has satisfied himself that the test results do indeed tell against it rather than against some other hypotheses also at work in the experiment.

Popper is not satisfied with the suggestion that an hypothesis must be independently testable if it is not to be dismissed as *ad hoc*. He admits that independent testability is a necessary condition if an hypothesis is to avoid being *ad hoc*, but he denies that it is sufficient. Popper proposes that in addition an hypothesis must *pass* the independent tests in question, for unless we do this, any hypothesis at all can be made independently testable by linking it in some way with "any testable but not yet tested fantastic *ad hoc* prediction which may occur to us (or to some science fiction writer)."[23] Whatever the merits may be of Popper's view that a good theory should *pass* some new, and severe, tests, the point I wish to make here is that if a theory is denounced as *ad hoc* because it *fails* the new and severe tests, the connection drawn earlier between the *ad hoc* hypothesis and closed-mindedness cannot be established here. We cannot tell from the fact that a proposed hypothesis in fact fails new tests that the person who proposed it did so merely to protect some favoured hypothesis from refutation. Conversely, a scientist who proposes a fantastic *ad hoc* hypothesis in a closed-minded attempt to hang on to some other hypothesis might in fact, amazingly enough, propose a hypothesis which passes new and severe tests. His success does not alter the fact that he was not prepared to abandon his position if the hypothesis had failed.

4/   A link with education?

Having attempted then to answer the objection that open-mindedness is logically impossible, and the objection that it clashes with other desirable attitudes, let us return more directly to the question of its positive educational value. Typically, open-mindedness is thought to be connected in some way with education but the nature of this connection is rarely spelled out.[24]

(a)   Contingent?
The connection might be thought of as *instrumental* inasmuch as a person who is independently found to be open-minded might also be found to be more capable of certain intellectual tasks and learning activities than a person with a closed mind. If such tasks and activities were held to be valuable, then the attitude of open-mindedness could be regarded as having instrumental value in that it makes such tasks and activities possible. The discovery of empirical connections of this kind is a task for social science, and psychologists such as Milton Rokeach have made important discoveries in this area.[25]

(b)   Necessary?
We can also inquire, however, whether or not there is any necessary connection between our idea of the educated person

and the concept of open-mindedness. If there were such a connection, then the attitude of open-mindedness would not simply be valued because it *leads on* to other things of value, i.e., it would not simply be valued as a means (though it could still be valued as such), but it would also be valued for its own sake. An investigation of such necessary connections is, of course, philosophical in character. If open-mindedness is a necessary condition of education, then to say that a person is educated is at once to say that he has an open mind.

Let us look immediately at a view, expressed by a well-known author of a popular book on clear thinking, which is apparently at odds with the suggestion that there is any such necessary link. Referring to prejudice, Thouless writes: "Education does not in itself save us from this disability. It ought to help us in the direction of freedom from prejudice, but it does not necessarily do so. Learned men are often as bound by their prejudices as anyone else."[26] A number of points need to be made here.

(i) If we use "education" to mean "schooling" (and there is some evidence elsewhere that Thouless does at times use it thus),[27] then, of course, there is no necessary link between education and open-mindedness. A school may well be a centre of propaganda and indoctrination.

(ii) The point might also be that even if a school attempts to dispel prejudice, it may be unsuccessful. Thus "it does not necessarily do so" may simply mean that attempts to teach can carry no guarantees of success with them.

(iii) Again if we identify the concepts of "educated" and "learned" (as Thouless apparently does above) then again it will follow that there is no necessary link with open-mindedness. For "learned" means that a person is in possession of a certain amount of knowledge or learning, and does not tell us what *attitude* the person has to the claims of knowledge which he makes.

On the other hand, we do not invariably use "education" as synonymous with "schooling" or with "learning"—we often use it precisely to distinguish some kinds of learning from others. We ask at times: "Your son is learning a lot, but is he getting an education?" or "Is this school really an *educational* institution?" In other words, we sometimes use the concept of education in a more restricted way. Consider this difference. It may be foolish but it is not nonsensical to set about *learning*, regardless of whether or not what we learn is true. But it is queer indeed to propose to set about *educating* ourselves, regardless of whether or not what we learn is true. Is not the reason for this oddity the fact that education necessarily involves a concern to distinguish the true from the false (and the reasonable from the unreasonable, etc.)? This is not to say that the views of an educated person actually *are* true, for the educated astronomer in the fourteenth century had very many false beliefs, and the twentieth-century astronomer may well have also. But the educated person is trying to sort out the true and the false, and indeed *cares* about the distinction.[28] But as we have seen, open-mindedness is the name of that attitude which continually strives to be open to counter-arguments to the beliefs which we hold. It involves being willing to consider objections to our own position and being willing to revise it in the face of good counter-argument or evidence. If A is not willing to consider objections which others may have, can we say that he has a concern for truth? If he is not willing to revise his position, can we say that he is concerned to get things right? If we cannot say these things, this shows that open-mindedness is a *necessary* condition of the concern in question. It might be thought that a counter-example to these claims would be the case of a person who had reason to believe that the objections were all false. Would it be necessary for the person to consider them? The point is surely that if he has reason to believe them false, this must be because he has *already* considered them (or considered the views of experts whom he has reason to trust). He need not feel obliged to *reconsider* the issue.

To have a concern for truth then is to have the attitude of open-mindedness. This follows from the necessary condition above. If then an educated person is one who has a concern for truth, the attitude of open-mindedness will be a characteristic of that person. This follows from the transitivity of impli-cation. A implies B and B implies C, therefore A implies C. Open-mindedness is then necessarily an aim of education in-sofar as education involves the pursuit of truth and this will be true of all societies and not merely democracies.[29]

We have seen at the end of chapter 1 that the attitude of open-mindedness cannot sensibly be applied to certain logical principles, such as the principle of revision in the light of rele-vant counter-examples, for any attempt at open-mindedness with respect to such a principle would at once invoke that principle. With respect to certain claims, such as first-person phenomenalistic statements like "I am in pain," reconsidera-tion of the arguments and/or evidence for such claims is not appropriate because the claims do not rest upon argument and evidence. (We must indeed allow that some things can be known without evidence for otherwise nothing could be known. The chain of questions asking for our evidence would be endless.)[30] But with such exceptions noted, the attitude of open-mindedness can be properly regarded as that which is *appropriate* to knowledge claims in that it recognizes such claims for what they are, i.e., revisable in the light of counter-evidence and counter-argument. Thus we value open-mind-edness not just because we believe that it in fact permits unfettered inquiry and thus facilitates the emergence of new ideas but also because we see that it is the attitude which any-one who makes pretensions to knowledge *ought* to have.

As our discussion of the principle of tenacity should remind us, however, virtues have a way of turning into vices. Reck-lessness can easily replace courage. In some cases, it is a matter of taking the virtue too far. We can be *too* generous, and help others at the cost of impoverishing our own family. Perhaps we would speak of a person being too open-minded if he were willing to pay serious attention to imaginative, but quite im-plausible, speculation such as that a famous personality might have been kidnapped or murdered and his place taken by a clever impostor (cf., the film *The Prize*). One can reasonably demand *very strong* evidence if certain claims are to be taken seriously, or very strong counter-evidence if certain beliefs are to be reconsidered. We need to distinguish open-mindedness and naïvety; the sensational tabloids make handsome profits when people are unable to reject nonsense outright. On the other hand, philosophers are not to be charged with naïvety because they pay serious attention to paradoxes which people in general simply reject as obviously wrong. We know, of course, that fast runners can and do overtake slow runners in front of them, but it remains interesting and important to see *how* Zeno's paradox arises, and to attempt to resolve it. Open-mindedness here does not involve entertaining the idea that Zeno might be correct but rather in being willing to find out how he goes wrong.

Having argued that it is a necessary condition of being educated, it is perhaps worth noting that unlike *abilities* such as creativity and effective thinking, open-mindedness can be aimed at *in general* and not simply in relationship to a given subject or discipline. We cannot assume that creative ability in philosophy will guarantee that the person will do creative work in, say, science. As Hirst has said "the use of broad, general terms for these abilities serves in fact to unify misleadingly quite disparate achievements."[31] There may well be some "carry over" to other subject areas (transfer of training), but such links would have to be revealed in empirical research. Thus teachers do not aim at creativity *per se*, even though they may wish their pupils to be creative in mathematics, physics, literary criticism, etc. But open-mindedness is the name of an *attitude*, and once one realizes what it involves and begins to adopt it, there is no logical reason why one could not be open-minded about *any* of one's beliefs. Having said this, however, we must remember that there may be particular reasons why A will *not* achieve an open-minded outlook in some areas of his life. Religion may remain a blind spot, for example, because of indoctrination. Of course, A is not said to be open-minded about some issue with which he is not at all familiar and thus he must have some knowledge of philosophy if he is to be open-minded *about* philosophical issues (as opposed to approaching the study of philosophy as a beginner in an open-minded way). But whereas he cannot necessarily transfer his creative abilities in science to his knowledge of philosophy because different sorts of achievements are involved in the two areas, there is no reason in principle why he cannot transfer his open-minded scientific outlook to his knowledge of philosophy.

It is also clear that open-mindedness is not a sufficient condition of being educated. A can be open-minded with respect to whatever knowledge he may possess, but this may be minimal. A skilled craftsman who is not yet an educated man may be open-minded about his craft. And if we take the notion of educated to rule out narrow specialization, clearly the narrow specialist could be open-minded about his specialty. Thus the claim is not that open-mindedness is the sole aim of education. It is claimed here that it is a necessary aim of education. And it may be that it is an aim which will make possible the achievement of other aims, such as familiarity with a range of subjects, by breaking down resistance to new ideas. This suggestion, however, involves us in the complex question of open-mindedness in teaching, and to this we must now turn.

Open-mindedness and
the teacher

4

1/ Preliminary remarks

We may think of open-mindedness as characterizing a *way* of teaching or we may think of it as an aim of teaching. If we are right in thinking of open-mindedness as the appropriate attitude with respect to truth and as having intrinsic value, then we will hold not only that teachers will aim at developing this trait in their students, but will also aim at manifesting it in their work as teachers. We need, however, to look more closely at the relationship between methods and aims of teaching.

A tentative analysis of the concept of teaching might indicate that it involves the selection and use of various tactics or strategies to promote learning of certain kinds.[1] We do not label an instance of teaching open-minded or not simply on the basis of the actual outcome in terms of promoting, or failing to promote, open-mindedness. Of course, the reason why a student becomes a closed-minded individual may be that his teachers failed to manifest open-mindedness (or perhaps deliberately indoctrinated him). In connection with the failure to be an example of an open-minded person, we can surely agree with R. S. Peters' view that "methods and forms of organization in schools can never just be regarded as ways of promoting particular objectives. For schools are educational institutions, which means that everything that goes on must be regarded as something that can be learnt, as well as an aid to learning."[2] We cannot, of course, *infer* from the fact that pupils emerge from school with closed minds that their teachers failed to teach in an open-minded way. There may be many forces at work in the homes of the students, and in society at large, which make the open-minded attitudes of teachers ineffective. Similarly, we cannot infer that the achievement of open-mindedness by the students is the result of open-minded teaching. The students may well have reacted strongly against the blatant dogmatism of their teachers. Indeed, teachers who want to achieve open-mindedness in their students may, on occasion, calculate that what is needed is a strong dose of flagrant bias to shake the students out of their complacency.[3] If successful, what has happened here is that a highly biased presentation prompts the students to question and to challenge. The outcome is open-mindedness, but it would be absurd to describe the biased account as itself open-minded. It worked as a strategy precisely because it did not represent open-mindedness. This, it should be clear, is not to recommend flagrant bias as a teaching strategy in general. The suitability of a method depends very much upon particular circumstances, and this particular technique has many limitations.[4] Indeed, the point of Peters' remarks about methods is to raise a general doubt about such techniques. Students do not necessarily follow the example set by their teachers, but any practice followed by a teacher *may* itself become something which students learn to follow.

It is important then to ask what it would mean to be open-minded in our teaching if we are to be capable of choosing an open-minded approach which could serve as an example of the trait to our students. If we decide to depart from this approach on occasion, in the interests of stimulating our students *to* open-mindedness, we will at least know *that* we are departing from it, and will not misleadingly hail our new approach as itself being open-minded. We will then perhaps avoid the "paradox-mongering"[5] which, for example, has confused discussions of freedom, leading many to the bizarre conclusion that freedom is *really* constraint.

2/ The teacher as neutral chairman

Let us consider in the light of the above comments the method of teaching advocated by the Schools Council's Humanities Curriculum Project,[6] and associated with the writings of Lawrence Stenhouse.[7] He is reported to have remarked recently that the project might have been better called the problems and effects of teaching about controversial issues;[8] and certainly the recommendations about teaching made in this body of work *are* directed towards teaching in the area of controversy. The project "aimed at a form of discussion in which the teacher should be a neutral and impartial chairman and resource consultant."[9]

Before examining this model more closely, we must note Stenhouse's recent claim that the project advocated nothing and made no recommendations. He writes: "There was no assertion that the premises were *correct*. The intention was to state a position clearly enough for teachers to know whether they were interested in exploring its implications."[10]

I think this is inconsistent with the position maintained in his earlier work. He claims there that (1) controversial issues are important and should be considered in school; (2) there are *three* possible strategies which can be employed; and (3) that two of these are respectively impracticable and unacceptable, and scarcely tenable in practice. Point (1) above argues for *some* strategy and points (2) and (3) eliminate all other strategies save that of the neutral-teacher approach. Is this not to recommend the latter?[11] My criticisms, however, will be relevant even if the neutral-teacher approach is now understood not to be advocated, but merely advanced as "an interesting possibility."

Looking more closely at the model provided by Stenhouse, we should notice first that it states an *ideal* to which teachers might try to *approach*. He remarks without further argument or elaboration that "of course, no teacher can be neutral.

There are no perfect performances. No teaching of philosophy is perfectly philosophical."[12] I will simply say here that "of course" here assumes a consensus which does not in fact exist in the literature, and Stenhouse makes no attempt to deal with the powerful case made by Ennis against the "neutrality is impossible" position.[13] Secondly, in this model the teacher *qua* person is not neutral, and indeed Stenhouse claims that neutral chairmanship "only makes sense if the teacher *qua* person is not neutral."[14] I think we are justified in reading "makes sense" here as a *logical* remark (rather than as the claim that it is only a sensible practice), because elsewhere Stenhouse argues that a teacher *must* have commitments of his own.[15] He holds this because he believes that to teach controversial matters well a teacher must believe them to be *important*. But whatever the truth of the empirical assertion relating to teaching X well, it is obviously possible to think X important without having taken a stand on it. Thirdly, while the teacher is to be neutral with respect to the substantive issue, he is not to be neutral with respect to standards of argumentation, respect for evidence, and other aspects of rational inquiry.[16] Finally, the teacher "is not teaching neutrality so much as the nature of responsible commitment."[17] Thus neutrality is not the aim of the teaching in terms of the *students' learning*, but is a criterion for assessing *the way* in which the teacher has taught.

We can now ask in what respects this approach to teaching can be regarded as open-minded. This, *in fact*, is how Stenhouse described the approach. Let us note at once that the phrase "an open-minded teacher" admits of ambiguity for we may use the adjective here in a predicative way, in which case we are saying that A is a teacher *and* A is open-minded, or in an *attributive* way, in which case we say something about the way in which A teaches.[18] In the first case we may find independently that A is an open-minded person and later that he is in fact a teacher. These facts would not jointly suffice to show that he was, in the attributive sense, an open-minded teacher, for while he may *hold* his beliefs in an open-minded way he may fail to *present* them to his students in an open-minded way. (We will examine later how such a failure might occur.) While both of these interpretations are possible, the second is more commonly the meaning of the phrase "an open-minded teacher." The first might occur in a context in which teachers as a group in society were known to be generally closed-minded on a host of issues. In such a context we might say "A is an open-minded teacher" and mean to call attention to the fact that *though* he is a teacher, he is an open-minded person, cf. "A is an open-minded politician." In a context, however, in which teachers may or may not be open-minded people, the comment that A is an open-minded teacher would surely suggest that we are saying something about A *qua* teacher. It is a comment on the way in which A sets about the task of teaching.

It is clear that Stenhouse also means to use "neutral" attributively when he speaks of the neutral-teacher; thus in identifying neutrality with open-mindedness, he is clearly referring to the way in which the teacher *goes about his task*. Still, there remains a possible source of confusion because it might be that Stenhouse regards this approach as open-minded (a) just because he thinks that being neutral in the classroom on a controversial issue means to be open-minded about it or (b) because he thinks that to be neutral is in fact the best way of fostering open-mindedness in students. Let us consider these possibilities in turn.

(a) Neutral-teaching as open-minded teaching

As we have seen earlier in our discussion of neutrality, the open-minded attitude sometimes involves being neutral but it does not demand this. It can be shown that the concepts are not equivalent because there are occasions on which a person is both non-neutral *and* open-minded about X. That Linus Pauling has come to the conclusion that Vitamin C is effective in inhibiting the onset of the common cold and is therefore no longer neutral on this issue, by no means *implies* that he has closed his mind to the arguments of the opposition, nor that he is unwilling to revise his view.

It is somewhat frustrating to read in a review of the Humanities Curriculum Project that "to the philosophers of education neutrality was a provocative word,"[19] as if the objection to Stenhouse were purely verbal. Stenhouse is not being convicted of linguistic confusion—neutrality is the correct word to describe the action of not taking sides. But he is involved in conceptual confusion if he thinks that the taking of sides necessarily implies being unwilling to revise one's position. Stenhouse correctly sees that the deliberate use of propaganda conflicts with open-minded teaching, but he misleadingly suggests that this shows that the teacher must be *neutral* if he is to be open-minded: "'Neutrality' means that the teacher should not propagate his own view, but be prepared to see the pupils treat all views according to consistent critical principles."[20]

The appropriate reply here is that the rejection of propaganda does not force us to adopt neutrality; and the open-minded support of a particular view by the teacher is perfectly consistent with having the pupils treat all views according to consistent *critical* principles. It is the *critical* principle that the false must be rejected which obliges the teacher to cast a particular view in a certain light. It is a mistake to identify neutrality with open-mindedness; and if neutral teaching is adopted *because* it is thought necessarily to be open-minded, then a mistaken *model* of open-mindedness is being presented to the students. If a case can be made for neutrality in teaching in the area of controversial issues, and this must be considered later, it cannot be made on the grounds that this is the only way of being open-minded. Finally, following the point made in chapter 2, section 4, we should not think that open-minded teaching can occur only in the teaching of controversial issues.

(b) Neutral-teaching for open-mindedness
There is some reason to think that Stenhouse may believe that neutral-teaching is open-minded teaching because it offers the best prospect of *producing* open-minded people. This is, of course, to claim an empirical connection and it is significant, for example, that Stenhouse castigates Mary Warnock and John Wilson for trying "to settle the question of the potential

of a teaching stance disciplined by the criterion of neutrality without allowing their minds to be clouded by looking at the available evidence."[21] In short, Stenhouse evidently believes that the approach is to be assessed in terms of its *results*, and these can be discovered only in an empirical investigation.

This is not to say that Stenhouse is open to the immediate objection that a student can become open-minded though his teacher was not, or that an open-minded teacher may fail to produce open-minded students. He quite properly notes that "the generalizations of the testing programme mask the variability of unique classroom situations. They cannot be taken as predictive of the effects of attempting to implement the neutral chairman role. Rather they must be regarded as indicating the potential without predicting that the potential will be reached in any given case."[22] Thus his claim would be that this method is more *likely* to achieve the desired outlook than any other method and it is therefore reasonable to adopt it.

We cannot, I think, immediately dismiss this suggestion on the grounds that a model of teacher neutrality might work against the desired objective of open-mindedness in the students. It *might*, but whether it would *in fact* cannot be answered *a priori*. And we could try to prevent such a result by explaining to students that being *neutral* is *not* the same as being open-minded. (Still, one wonders why students who can appreciate the point that a teacher might have to adopt method X in order to teach them attitude Y, could not similarly appreciate that a teacher who, for whatever reason, *lectures* to them does not thereby show that he wants the students to take his *word* for the truth of the claims he makes.)

When one turns to look at the available empirical research *to which Stenhouse refers us*, the results seem quite inconclusive. This is how two researchers personally state their conclusion:

> the major finding is that no marked deterioration in the attitudinal or personality characteristics of the pupils was manifested in their test responses after exposure to the programme. The effects of the experiment, although

not generally significant, tended to suggest a shift in the direction of inter-ethnic tolerance.[23]

And further on they write:

there is no evidence to suggest that the students generally become less sensitive to or tolerant of members of other racial groups.[24]

On the one hand then the neutral approach does not seem to be harmful and on the other there is a *suggestion* that it *may* promote tolerance. Apart from these inconclusive findings, however, we need to call attention to other aspects of the research. (1) There was no formal follow-up evaluation of the experiment.[25] This would appear to be a serious shortcoming inasmuch as trait-names refer to *ongoing* dispositions to act in certain ways. (2) It is not at all clear that these findings are directly relevant to the notion of open-mindedness, for this concept is not *as such* discussed but rather the concepts of tolerance and prejudice. (3) There appears to have been no *comparative* study of other teaching approaches, for example, discussion methods in which the teacher does take a stand at times in an open-minded way, and other methods, such as formal instruction. In the absence of such comparative data, we can hardly conclude that the neutral approach is *more likely* to produce open-minded people than other approaches, even if the research suggests that it may promote open-mindedness. Indeed, as we will see later in chapter 6, Stenhouse and others appear to hold that other methods are *in principle* at odds with open-minded teaching. But this issue must be shelved for now.

Whether or not neutral-teaching can claim to be open-minded teaching because it is the most effective method of fostering open-mindedness in students remains then an open question. The comparative research has not been undertaken. The practical importance of recognizing that this particular issue is empirical and not philosophical is that the necessary research *will not* be undertaken if ideology persuades us that certain methods could not lead to students becoming open-minded. If we are persuaded that *in principle* method X could not foster open-mindedness, we may be in danger of dismissing counter-examples as necessarily spurious. We believe we know *a priori* that they must be false, and the belief becomes a matter of uncritically received dogma. In fact, however, the careful examination of alleged counter-examples remains necessary if we ourselves are to be open-minded about these claims.

3/ Criteria of open-minded teaching

Since we do *not* know as a matter of fact that being open-minded in our teaching is less effective than being neutral, let us try to be clearer about the meaning of being open-minded in our teaching not just for the sake of clarity, but in order that any future empirical research into this question may be based on a clear conception of open-minded teaching.

It will certainly be an aid to clarity in the discussion to follow if we can eliminate at once the suggestion that A cannot be an open-minded teacher (attributive sense) just because (a) he belongs to a certain political, religious, or ethnic group and (b) he holds certain beliefs. Since these beliefs still attract a following, it will be worth looking at two representative specimens in order to *show* that they are false. My argument can, of course, be generalized to *any* group or *any* set of beliefs.

(a) Group membership?

It is sometimes claimed that at times it is justifiable to exclude from the teaching profession persons who belong to certain organizations, on the grounds that *membership* of the particular group implies that the person cannot be an open-minded teacher. For example, Arthur Bestor claims that

> there is ... one perfectly valid ground for denying to a proved Communist the privilege of teaching in American college or school. ... He has repudiated the standards of scholarship in favour of the standards of a

political bureaucracy. He has abdicated intellectual responsibility and has rendered himself incapable of communicating to his students any genuine appreciation of critical, objective, disinterested thinking.[26]

Presumably one proves that a person is a Communist by showing that he is a member of the Communist party. But it is clearly fallacious to argue that a person cannot be open-minded (or objective, critical, and disinterested) simply because he is a member of a party. It is possible for example, to join a party in order to work for its destruction from within.[27] We cannot infer that a person has a closed mind from the fact that he is a member of a party which favours closed-mindedness, for there can be a whole variety of reasons which explain why the person is a member, which have nothing to do with party doctrine. Two further points need to be made: (i) If a person belongs to a party which insists that it has the right to determine what is true, then even if the person believes this it does not follow that his classroom teaching will reflect his belief. (ii) If the teacher does attempt to convey this belief to his students, it does not follow that he must do so in a closed-minded manner. What both of these points show is that the possession of certain beliefs does not logically exclude open-mindedness, and that what we must concern ourselves with is the *actual performance* of the teacher. If we are to take action against him, it is because we have *independent* evidence of his use of propaganda, and not because we suspect he may use propaganda because other members of his group have used it.[28]

(b) Particular beliefs?

One also meets the view that a lack of religious conviction, for example, prevents a person from being open-minded. Consider the following statement:

A secular professor trained in naturalism may enter upon his research with certain definite prejudices. For example, here is a professor of psychology who is sure there is no spiritual soul, although he has no evidence for that conviction. His research is conditioned by blind irrational prejudice. The Catholic professor trained in metaphysics enters his laboratory with no such bias.[29]

The "may" in the first sentence suggests that the secular professor's training could prove to be an obstacle to open-minded inquiry *in fact*; but the final sentence, introducing a contrast with the Catholic researcher, tends to suggest that *only* the latter background permits unbiased inquiry. If we take the claim in the latter sense, then the reply is surely that there is no reason in principle why a professor who has been trained in tradition X could not regard the beliefs of that tradition as subject to revision. A specific set of beliefs, e.g., secularism, does not logically rule out open-mindedness; and a specific set of beliefs, e.g., Catholicism, does not logically guarantee open-mindedness. This is an attempt to suggest that open-mindedness is impossible for all save those who subscribe to a specific set of beliefs, the latter being both necessary and sufficient for open-mindedness. And we have seen earlier that this is false.

4/ Open-mindedness in teaching

These erroneous suggestions, however, serve to remind us that when we use "open-minded" attributively in the phrase "an open-minded teacher" we are making a comment about the way in which the teacher goes about his or her task. But the phrase "the way in which A teaches" which I have used up to this point requires more attention. Does it, for example, refer to (a) specific procedures to be followed by the teacher, i.e., particular actions he is to perform, or to (b) a manner, style, or attitude in teaching, i.e., the way in which he carries out certain actions or the attitude which he displays towards what he does, or does it perhaps refer to both of these?

(a) Specific procedures
Teaching is a polymorphous concept[30] which refers to many activities including giving explanations, referring to sources,

discussing issues, etc., and these are activities which may or may not be conducted in an open-minded way. For example, a teacher might offer an explanation which deliberately ignores or distorts an alternative theory.

We would surely say that an open-minded teacher is one who, *among other things*, entertains criticisms of his opinions which the students may have, looks at sources which conflict with the view he is defending, if there are any such, indicates where he thinks flaws may be found in his argument. We cannot, however, claim that such procedures are invariably necessary if our teacher is not to be closed-minded, for there is a variety of reasons which could justify or explain the absence of these or similar actions. For example, the teacher may not be able to think of any possible flaws in an argument; there may be no time to listen to a criticism if there is a more urgent objective; or there may be no sources which disagree with some well-corroborated theory. (If there are, the teacher may not know of them.)

On the other hand, in particular contexts, any one of these could be necessary. Thus, if some controversial issue is being discussed, open-minded teaching demands that views which conflict with those of the teacher *not* be excluded. As John Stuart Mill put it, "Both teachers and learners go to sleep at their post as soon as there is no enemy in the field."[31] It is not enough that the teacher may have considered the contrary views personally in an open-minded way. We would not regard his teaching as open-minded here unless he drew the attention of the students to the views which he rejects and attempted to *explain* why he rejects them.

There is, however, a danger of falsely concluding that when such a necessary condition has been met, open-mindedness in teaching is assured; but this is to confuse a necessary with a sufficient condition. Consider the following recommendation which includes the examination of contrary views:

> In the sort of school which conforms to the requirements of the Church and Christian parents, one will not find this obvious drawback to education, that the doctrines

which the pupils have learned in their religious instruction are contradicted in the teaching of the other subjects. And if teachers think it proper, in the interests of education, to draw attention to books tainted with error for the purpose of refuting them, they will use such precautions and supply such an effectual antidote of true doctrine that the Christian education of their pupils will suffer no detriments but rather gain advantage from the process.[32]

The necessary condition of looking at contrary views is satisfied here, and yet it is clear that this teaching falls far short of open-mindedness (quite apart from the actual *outcome* of the teaching). This *approach* fails to be open-minded, not because the teacher is defending a particular position, for positions can be defended in both open- and closed-minded ways; and not because the teacher sets out to refute the positions which he regards as erroneous, for refutations can be conducted in both open- and closed-minded fashion; it fails because "precautions" are taken to try to *ensure* that a particular outcome will be reached. This is incompatible with the open consideration of the contrary view. The use of the metaphor "antidote" is also revealing, for the teacher is not to limit himself to the use of rational argument, but is prepared to try to condition the child. We need to look beyond the appearances, and to ask exactly how the conflicting views are being presented and treated.

In addition to the philosophical point that the deliberate attempt to prevent someone from seriously considering the alternative viewpoint violates the concept of open-minded inquiry, there is empirical evidence that the examination of contrary views can be a valuable aid to the would-be propagandist or indoctrinator. Research shows that people are more likely to discount future counter-arguments if those arguments have been mentioned, or anticipated, by the propagandist in his presentation. Following on with the "antidote" metaphor, researchers often refer to this technique as "inoculation." The listener is no longer caught by surprise by a counter-argument and its impact is minimized.[33] The ulterior motives in these cases defeat the ascription of open-mindedness.

(b) Manner, style, and attitude

(i) *Failure through self-deception.* To have the attitude of an open-minded teacher is just to be willing or disposed to do the sorts of things which would count as open-minded teaching, such as entertaining criticism, considering conflicting sources, indicating possible flaws, revising one's view and so on. How then, we might ask, could an open-minded person possessed of teaching skills fail to be an open-minded teacher? The qualification "possessed of teaching skills" is necessary, because an open-minded person might not be able to teach *at all* and *a fortiori* could not then be an open-minded teacher. Let us also ignore the case of the open-minded person possessed of teaching skills who does not *try* to be an open-minded teacher. We will focus on the case of the individual who tries to be an open-minded teacher. Can this person fail?

One such case is that of *self-deception.* A is open-minded about issue X, knows how to present such an issue in an open-minded way, *intends* to be open-minded in the classroom, but in the event fails. Listening to a tape-recording of the lesson, he himself may realize that, although at the time he *believed* he was willing to listen seriously to an objection, he was not in fact willing to do so. It is clear to him from the evidence of what he had to say, and how he said it, that he was not disposed to consider an alternative view. His sincerity is not in question, and he does not deserve the censure of the man who merely pretends to be open-minded. He had, in short, deceived himself, for as has been noted of tolerance, "a man may conceal not only from others but also from himself the inward intolerance that lies behind his outward tolerance."[34] Superficially our teacher may have gone through the motions of entertaining objections and replying, but he now realizes that he had not been willing to consider revising his views. (My case is not exactly the same as the tolerance example because in the latter the man is deceived *in general*. In my case, the man is truly an open-minded person, but deceives himself *on occasion* into thinking that he is willing to revise his views when he is not.)[35]

(ii) *Unconscious bias?* On the other hand, I do not think we would be inclined to say that a teacher had not been open-minded just because on objective grounds one could show that his account of an issue was in fact lacking in objectivity or was biased in some way. This would be *evidence* for the view that he was not being open-minded, if we thought that it revealed that he was not willing to consider an alternative account fairly. But bias is not always a matter of conscious intent.[36] We can judge a work in history or politics to be biased, knowing nothing of the author's intentions and without ascribing any such intention to the author. Notice too that we say such things as, "I will try to be fair but I may be biased because ..." and then cite a fact which may, for all our care, produce a slanted view. It may indeed be that bias is "often and even characteristically unconscious."[37] (We take "characteristically" here to mean "typically" rather than "necessarily," for conscious bias is certainly possible.) The open-minded teacher will, of course, *try* to eliminate bias; it is therefore important to be aware that bias can slip into our teaching unawares, for without this awareness we would have a false sense of security.

A person then can properly be regarded as teaching in an open-minded way if *trying* to avoid bias, even though his actual account falls short of being impartial. On the other hand, if the teacher has such a poor grasp of the sorts of specific steps he can take to reduce bias that his account is grossly distorted, there will come a point when the description "open-minded" can no longer be seriously applied to his teaching. Thus objective considerations do come in *at some point*. But it is not *every* objective failure which will cause the description to be removed. When Montefiore writes, "a biased report or position of any kind is quite simply one that fails of impartiality, objectivity or open-mindedness,"[38] he should be understood, I believe, as maintaining not that a biased report necessarily fails of open-mindedness, but that this is *one* of the standards it may fall short of. Cases of conscious bias fail in this way. (Further problems concerning bias will be considered when we look at the teaching of certain subjects in chapter 5.) A teacher will then not be denied the ascription of open-mindedness simply because he slips into a biased report.

(iii)   *Manner and style?* It is one thing, however, to *have* a certain attitude or disposition and another to be perceived as having that attitude or disposition. We are sometimes surprised to hear that A does not like our attitude, when we can honestly claim not to have that attitude at all. Suppose I try as a teacher to *convey* to my students that I am open-minded about the issues under investigation, may I not fail? Is it not possible that they will see me as pretending, as a phoney? May I not come across to them as dogmatic and closed-minded? It is here, of course, that my manner and style may give the lie to my real attitude. Since the judgment that A is or is not open-minded is an inference we make from certain behaviour it is clearly possible that mistakes can be made. Now if A is perceived by his students as being dogmatic and closed-minded, though he is not in fact dogmatic and closed-minded, are we to describe him as an open-minded teacher or not?

On the one hand, it seems odd to hail A as an open-minded teacher when he is universally detested by his students who label him dogmatic. And yet we do not want to settle the question of A's open-mindedness as a teacher by head-counting. It may be the students' own closed-mindedness which prevents them from entertaining the idea that a teacher, who, for example, defends a certain view, could be open-minded. The objective and subjective assessments clash again—objectively, A is being open-minded, but he does not *seem* to be.

What we must say, I think, is simply that A's teaching *is* open-minded inasmuch as he *is* willing to consider objections, revise his views, etc., but that he is not able to present himself *as* an open-minded individual teacher *to these particular students*. He cannot succeed in setting an example of open-mindedness which they can appreciate. This may or may not be his fault. Perhaps in a particular set of social conditions, no one could set an example of open-mindedness which would be seen as such, for it could be that only a closed-minded approach would be regarded as open-minded. For example, if one identifies open-mindedness with a particular set of beliefs, the dogmatic indoctrination of those beliefs might be thought to be open-minded teaching. On the other hand, it may be that while the teacher *is* willing to revise his views he cannot succeed in creating the *impression* that he is so willing because he lacks the ability to communicate with students. Legitimate criticisms of his style and manner may be made. Compare here the phrase "an interesting teacher." Suppose that a person as a teacher takes a variety of steps, such as introducing contemporary material, bringing in guest speakers, etc., in order to create interest in his secondary school students, but something in his manner puts them off and they remain bored. From one point of view we want to say that as a teacher he *is* doing interesting things — other things being equal, this approach ought to interest the students. But on the other hand, the undeniable fact is that he is not succeeding in winning the interest of the students. The point is that teaching can be assessed to some extent in objective terms (assuming that we are in a position to make such an assessment), e.g., he *is* willing to revise his views, he is not merely repeating material already well-worn. A teacher, however, is always a teacher *to* some particular people. (The parallel between "open-minded" and "interesting" is not exact because, unlike "open-minded," "interesting" carries the preposition "to" with it.) What we must say is that A *is* an open-minded teacher even though he is *thought* not to be; but if through some fault of his own he cannot communicate this attitude, it may be held that he is not a suitable teacher in these particular circumstances, assuming that it is a model of open-mindedness which we wish to set. If action were taken against him it would not, of course, be on the same basis as action against the propagandist. It would be on the grounds that his manner or style fail to manifest the attitude which he actually has, and in the *pedagogical* context this can be a serious shortcoming.

5/ Is teaching necessarily open-minded?

One sometimes meets the view that when the concept of teaching is properly satisfied, so too is the concept of open-minded teaching. This view is found to some extent in the writings of those, notably Israel Scheffler, who identify "teaching" and "rational explanation." Sometimes this view presents itself as a *value* judgment about the role teachers *ought* to fulfil.

The teacher in a free society is not just a technician. ... He needs a basic flexibility of mind, a capacity to step outside his subject and consider it from without together with his student, a fundamental respect for his student's mind, and a willingness to encourage new ideas, doubts, questions and puzzlements.[39]

On the other hand, it is sometimes found as a *conceptual* claim about what it means to *teach*. Thus Scheffler writes:

Teaching may be characterized as an activity aimed at the achievement of learning and practised in such manner as to respect the student's intellectual integrity and capacity for independent judgment. Such a characterization ... differentiates the activity of teaching from such other activities as propaganda, conditioning, suggestion, and indoctrination, which are aimed at modifying the person but strive at all costs to avoid a genuine engagement of his judgment on underlying issues.[40]

The teacher, if he deserves that title, gives the student the best arguments he can produce, and ones which he himself finds plausible and persuasive. He maintains a critical and reflective stance towards his own views.

This view is generally dismissed as obviously false, and indeed it seems that there are cases in which we do employ the concept of teaching when such attitudes are not necessarily involved. We do, for example, *teach* a dog to perform tricks or to obey commands. On the other hand, it is odd to apply the concept of *teaching* in some contexts in which no reasons can be offered for one's view. If A has an ultimate commitment and can offer no reason at all in support of his view, we speak of passing on or inculcating the view but *teaching* it sounds odd. Again, when explanations are unnecessary as, for example, in learning someone's name or address, the notion of teaching does not seem applicable. But when a child is learning his own name for the first time and is being brought to understand the practice of having names, the oddity in talk of teaching disappears. Thus there appears to be something in the view that at times we use "teach" in a more restricted way to imply explaining, reason-giving, etc., but it is not invariably so used and genuine instances of teaching occur in which such implications are not present.[41] Indeed, we have already seen how a teacher might decide to try to teach his students open-mindedness by teaching in a dogmatic way. One cannot say then that teaching is open-minded by definition, though one may well maintain that teaching ought to be open-minded. In the final chapter of this book we will look at the views of those who are opposed to open-mindedness in teaching. More immediately we must turn to consider the arguments of those who urge that open-mindedness is impossible in the teaching of certain subjects and that open-mindedness is ruled out by certain teaching methods and ensured by others.

Open-mindedness and subject areas

5

1/ Preliminary remarks

We looked in chapter 3 at the view that open-mindedness is in principle impossible. It was argued there that this view rests on confusion, namely the belief that any new experience must be forced into our already existing conceptual framework. Apart from the fact that we can alter our conceptual framework, even if we utilize the conceptual framework which we possess there is room for open-mindedness because it may not be clear how or where the new experience is to be fitted in. The empirical evidence is that we can usefully distinguish those who are more and those who are less open-minded, understanding the terms open- and closed-minded to suggest extremes along a continuum rather than all or nothing categories.[1]

In chapter 4 we saw how it is sometimes maintained that particular individuals *cannot* be (not just *are not*) open-minded because they belong to a certain group or have a particular set of beliefs. In this chapter we will look at the view that open-mindedness is impossible in the teaching of certain *subjects*. There is, it is held, something in the nature of the subject being taught which makes open-mindedness not just difficult but logically impossible. The first such argument is, in fact, a variant of that which holds that the possession of certain beliefs excludes open-mindedness, but it is included here because it is typically employed in the context of teaching in a particular area, namely religious beliefs.

The objections to be considered attempt to show that the impossibility of open-mindedness is logical in nature. If the arguments employed to this end can be shown to be fallacious, then it will make sense at least to look for ways in which present impossibilities of an empirical kind, and general difficulties, might be overcome. Philosophy's contribution here is to enable us to determine whether or not there is any point in investigating such ways of overcoming the problems.

Naturally an exhaustive examination of all objections in this area is not possible, but I propose to look at a variety of arguments which continue to be employed by large numbers of people. When I examine an objection to the possibility of open-mindedness with special reference to a particular area, it should be realized that a similar objection might be, and often is, raised in connection with the teaching of other subjects. Here I will examine the arguments that certain subjects contain assumptions which cannot be challenged, that bias is inevitable in some subjects, that conditioning determines our value judgments, and finally that any differentiation of subject areas destroys open inquiry.

2/ Must some questions necessarily be closed?

The 1944 Education Act in Great Britain declared that religious instruction shall be given in every county school. Provincial legislation in Canada too has often required that respect for religion and the precepts of Christian morality be inculcated by means of school lessons.[2] Those who teach in the area of religion have had to face up to the accusation that their lessons would be more accurately labelled religious indoctrination. Whether or not this charge was always fair, it has led to a reconsideration and restatement of objectives in religious education. For example, a Schools Council pamphlet holds that religious education "is a process whereby ultimate questions are kept open, not a process of trying to close them."[3] A later Schools Council working paper on religious education reminds us that "education thrives on the airing of conflicting viewpoints in a common desire to let truth prevail."[4]

To some extent it would be fair to say that this has become the dominant view in Britain and Canada, though many remain sceptical about how far traditional attitudes among teachers of religion have really altered.[5] Even supposing that attitudes have changed, to what extent is an open-minded approach a practical possibility? For example, will the students not realize that the truth of Christianity is presupposed by the school?[6] Without minimizing the practical problems we should not, I think, be inclined to regard them as insuperable before we have at least tried to implement certain imaginative strategies which might overcome them.[7]

Our main concern here, however, must be with the suggestion that there is *in logic* some reason why an open-minded approach is impossible. Reacting to a typical statement of what I have termed the dominant view, in which a minister of religion rejected an "inducting type of religious education" and called for an open inquiry into religious views, Lionel Elvin asked: "Merely as a matter of reasonable use of terms (and without any argument either way) can a person who is so 'open' as to doubt whether there is a God who is a person, be described as a Christian? Is the question of the existence of a God ... open or closed?"[8] Let us grant here that if A is a Christian, it follows that he does believe in a God who is a person, ignoring disputes about the possibility of using "Christian" in other ways. The point then is that if A is a Christian, this particular question is not an open question *for him* because he has made up his mind. He does not doubt the existence of God, for inasmuch as he is a Christian, he has such a belief.

But why should this be thought to constitute an obstacle to open-minded teaching? In the first place, we need to point out that although A does not doubt the existence of God, he may well be open-minded enough to listen seriously to the objections of those who either have doubts or who do not believe at all. Thus A may teach in this open-minded way. Secondly, even if A *personally* regards this matter as decisively settled, there is no reason why *as a teacher* he could not present it as a matter of ongoing controversy to his students. I do not think that we can make it part of the meaning of "Christian" that such a presentation is ruled out.[9] Finally, even if A argues for the truth of his position in the classroom, open-minded teaching does not necessarily disappear. The teacher may attempt to set out the alternatives in a full and fair way. He may try to ensure that his students are not won over because he is in a position of authority. He may, in addition, be very willing to listen to objections and criticisms which the students have. As Ninian Smart has said, "It is one thing to present a faith sympathetically but openly (that is, by showing an appreciation of the alternatives to it); it is quite another to teach people that it is true while remaining silent or prejudiced about alternatives."[10] Elvin in fact fallaciously infers that if the approach is to be open, then we will come to a *neutral* approach in religious education: "If it is agreed that the discussion be open in this sense then it is more likely that we shall be teaching *about* religion than engaging in the teaching *of* religion."[11] Presumably the point here is that if one is teaching *about* X, one is *not* taking a stand on the question of the truth or falsity of X, but one is perhaps trying to develop an *understanding* of X. This is a valuable point to make, insofar as it is often assumed (as we will see in chapter 6 when we look at teaching methods) that teaching necessarily implies preaching. But it is quite false to suggest that neutrality is the only alternative to preaching. It is a separate and debatable question to what extent neutrality is the most desirable stance; but we should at least recognize that the open-minded teaching *of* religion is yet another alternative to evangelizing and propaganda.

Indeed, earlier in his paper Elvin himself provides the distinction which we need here to appreciate how the teaching of religion X can be open. Attacking the unjust state of affairs in which Christians have control of religious education although our society is pluralistic, he comments: "It should not call for much analytical power to distinguish between expressing an opinion as to what one thinks is right and implying that one's own view is the only one that can be thought right."[12] This is a genuine distinction, and if we apply it to the case of the Christian who is a teacher, it is clear how the concept of open-mindedness has room to operate. This is not, of course, to say that it will *in fact* be possible to avoid distortion, bias, and evangelizing in the teaching situation. And this is the starting point of the second popular objection.

3/ The ever-present danger argument

Although this form of argument crops up in discussions of the teaching of religion, history, and literature, I will illustrate it here from the context of teaching the social sciences. We have seen in chapter 4 that bias may be conscious or unconscious, and that when unconscious bias enters into one's teaching we do not necessarily conclude that the teacher has failed to be open-minded. We do expect the open-minded teacher to treat issues fairly and this means that he must *attempt* to avoid bias, but some unintentional bias will be tolerated before the ascription of open-mindedness is withdrawn. The argument before us now, however, suggests that this attempt is pointless because bias and prejudice *inevitably* enter into our thinking in the social sciences; *a fortiori*, they inevitably enter into any teaching in this area. Bias here does not simply mean favouring a particular side, but rather adopting a position which is not warranted on the evidence. It fails to be objective and involves personal preferences and interests. This view is now so much a part of the accepted and dominant ideology that it is not easy to track down someone who *defends* it, as opposed to someone who merely *asserts* it or assumes it. But such a case is provided by the work of Howard Becker. He maintains that it is not possible to do sociological research "that is uncontaminated by personal and political sympathies"[13] and also that "there is no position from which sociological research can be done that is not biased in one way or another"[14]. If this is correct, the attempt to be open-minded is clearly a hopeless task—any revision of our work would only replace one bias with another. Rational reconsideration becomes impossible.

In a later reply to a critique by Gresham Riley,[15] Becker insists that he meant that sociologists cannot avoid being subjected to the *charge* of being biased—in the sense that the research is seen as favouring one side or another in a controversy.[16] Now even if this were true, it would not show, as Riley makes clear in his own reply, that the research *is* biased but only that it has been *called* biased.[17] Moreover, as Becker's use of the word "probably" indicates (when he writes that "the most objective ... research imaginable will probably be accused of bias"),[18] it does not *necessarily follow* that such charges will be made.

We need to point out that supporting a particular side, though it often leads to the charge of bias being made, does not entail that the view *is* biased in any pejorative sense, for a person may very fairly evaluate the evidence and reach a justifiable conclusion. And one can remain open-minded about the conclusion so reached. For the charge of bias to be sustained, it must be shown how the work is biased, otherwise the charge is empty. But then, if the biased elements are uncovered, why is it *in principle* impossible to remove them? It appears that Becker's reason for thinking that bias cannot be removed is as follows. In his original paper, he raises the possibility that we might be able to so conduct our research that it would *run counter* to our own biases, but then he asks: "Given all our techniques of theoretical and technical control, how can we be sure that we will apply them impartially and across the board as they need to be applied? Our textbooks in methodology are no help here. They tell us how to guard against error, but they do not tell us how to make sure that we will use all the safeguards available to us."[19] But against this it may be argued:

(a)   Possession of techniques does not guarantee that we will utilize those techniques to make *discoveries*, for example, but we do sometimes utilize them in fact to make discoveries.

(b) Although we cannot know in advance that we will succeed in remaining unbiased, we can know in looking at our work in retrospect that we have succeeded in being unbiased.

(c) The fact that we cannot *guarantee* that our work will not turn out to be biased is not the same as saying that it *must* turn out to be biased. It does not follow that we are *bound* to be closed-minded because we are always in *danger* of being closed-minded, anymore than we are bound to be mistaken because we are always liable to make mistakes. Our dealer cannot be certain that the car we purchase will be trouble-free, but this does not ensure that we will have problems. It is true that it is always possible that we will slip into bias even when we are trying to guard against it, but this does not show that in writing or teaching social science we cannot avoid bias.[20] To be unable to avoid the possibility of bias is not to be unable to avoid bias itself. Thus it has not been shown that it is pointless to aim at avoiding or eliminating bias.

4/ Cultural conditioning—the case of music

It is very widely held that, in those areas of the curriculum, particularly aesthetic education, which involve value judgments, rational assessment is impossible. Although the following quotation is uncompromising, it is not, I think, unrepresentative of a powerful body of opinion in educational circles. Referring to "the social nature of musical taste," John Mueller writes of modern man: "Had he been reared in another culture, and in another epoch, his convictions would have been otherwise—but he would have been equally content with them. In fact, he might have been downright belligerent, even to the extent of liquidating those who believed otherwise."[21] Thus modern man's fond belief in his own superior taste and tolerance is exposed as the inevitable product of social conditioning from infancy.

It is worth pausing to notice that while neither evidence nor argument is adduced by Mueller in support of this contention, it can readily be seen that the view is false. First, convictions in different cultures and epochs are not always, and again not necessarily, different. Second, people are not always, and certainly not necessarily, content with the views which are dominant in their own society. Third, even if A is content with the views which he has, it by no means follows that he must be closed-minded about them. He *might* be belligerent and many have been, but there is nothing *necessary* about this. Fourth, the existence of widespread divergence of musical preferences from one culture to another in itself cannot show that taste is necessarily a product of social conditioning, or that discussion of musical preferences is impossible.[22]

Mueller attempts to categorize the social forces which contribute to the formation of music norms, and it is in this discussion that a crucial fallacy in his thinking can be detected. He writes under the heading of one such force, namely "Technological factors": "Technological progress in metallurgy and instrument construction which made the valve instrument possible, permitted chromatic passages previously unplayable. We may, therefore, justifiedly state that the science of physics, for example, has influenced greatly the formation of our musical taste."[23] Physics has been influential here insofar as it has provided the *necessary* conditions for having certain experiences. But it cannot therefore be inferred that it has influenced our taste in the sense that it was sufficient to ensure that we would place a certain *value* on an experience. It is this latter claim which Mueller requires if the conditioning thesis is to be supported, but it is only the former claim which he has done anything to sustain. That which makes the formation of a view *possible* does not make the formation of that view *necessary*. Mueller, of course, lists other forces as contributing to the eventual conditioning and does not claim that physics is independently sufficient. My point is that he has done nothing to show that it even *contributes* to a conditioning process, though it may be necessary if a certain conditioning process is ever to occur. Precisely similar criticisms need to be made about his comments on "Biological factors."[24] Of course, if we had not heard the female voice (supposing that women sang with the same voice as men) we could not state a preference for it. But whereas Mueller correctly lists this as a limiting factor, he fails to see that it cannot support his conditioning thesis.

Mueller refers also to the influence of social heritage, a musical tradition, in the formation of our tastes, and to the influence of social factors such as patronage, institutions, and so on. And if the claim were simply that such factors may influence the formation of musical taste, there would be no basis for disagreement. But we are given no grounds for accepting that we are the helpless recipients of such stimuli. Traditions are often changed and sometimes abandoned. Dominant tastes in society are often attacked. Mueller asserts that "tastes *can* be accounted for; but once they are developed, they become non-rational and are not subject to rational defence or justification."[25] This, if true, would sound the death-knell of open-minded reflection, but what reason do we have to believe this? Reasons can be, and are, produced for one's musical preferences. Judgments about performances can be supported by reference to the performance itself. Mueller points out that we cannot prove these "correct or logical, in the natural science sense."[26] To this we need to ask why it should be thought that a test which is applicable in one area should be applicable in another area? And why one form of testing should dominate our notion of proof? Mueller adds: "By utilising the mechanical discoveries of Galileo and Edison, we can improve and accomplish what they would like to have achieved; by standing on the shoulders of Newton, we can enlarge our vision of the universe. But by standing on the shoulders of Shakespeare or Beethoven, we do not write a better play or compose a finer symphony than they."[27] Apart from the fact that this contradicts his own more accurate observation elsewhere that creative artists do profit from the work of their predecessors,[28] we can question the aptness of the comparison. Even if we are not enabled to write a finer symphony after hearing Beethoven, this does not show that we do not have an enhanced *appreciation* of what a symphony can be. And in the context of a discussion of musical taste, this is the important point.

The reader will readily find these kinds of arguments and others deployed in connection with the teaching of other subject areas; but it is time to turn to consider the contemporary view that the very differentiation of subjects into distinct kinds of knowledge is itself the source of closed-mindedness.

5/ The attack from "New Directions Sociology"

In recent years philosophers have devoted much energy to an attempt to determine: "whether the domain of objective experience and knowledge is, for example, one complex body of interrelated concepts, a unity of some sort, a number of similar forms of experience and knowledge with parallel relations between the concepts in each area, or whether it has some other implicit organization."[29] This inquiry has led to the view that there is in fact a number of logically distinct forms of knowledge.[30] Such a view is not, as such, at all new in philosophy, for Descartes argued that to make progress as a student of history was not thereby to make progress as a student of philosophy.[31] But the modern work has carried the detailed examination much further, and has raised the question of the relevance of the distinctions drawn for curriculum planning.

This philosophical work has come under attack in recent sociology of education for trying to set up as absolute distinctions what are said to be "no more than the socio-historical constructs of a particular time."[32] Thus *we* may distinguish between science and philosophy, but (a) other cultures may not do so; (b) other times did not always do so; and (c) we should realize that such distinctions are arbitrary, culturally relative, and largely the result of selfish motives.

Before examining the details of this critique, it would be well to distinguish it from two quite different positions. The first of these is the general criticism of traditional subject divisions in schools. It is clear that under the general subject heading of "English," questions of different kinds can be, and are, tackled, e.g., historical, literary, conceptual, and linguistic. (Compare also such subjects as "British Constitution," "Canadian Studies," and "Religious Education.") We can admit that these are socially constructed ways of organizing the curriculum and may misleadingly appear to be absolute categories. The philosopher's concern has been then with the forms of knowledge and not with the traditional school subjects[33] and this is in fact recognized by the sociologists.[34] The second critique not to be confused with the contemporary attack is that of John Dewey. His objection to teaching by way of fixed subject matter was that such classifications are foreign to the experience of the *child* and fail therefore to be meaningful to him. He was not attempting to show that the distinctions are illusory.

The importance of facing up to the contemporary sociological critique in this context can be seen by considering the following comment from this movement on the work of the Schools Council. This latter body is accused of modifying existing academic curricula without changing the existing social evaluation of knowledge: "by taking the assumptions of the academic curricula for granted, the social evaluations of knowledge implicit in such curricula are by implication being assumed to be in some sense 'absolute' and therefore not open to enquiry."[35] These remarks will need to be examined more carefully in due course; meanwhile we can note that it is charged that open-mindedness is lost because certain questions are not open for examination.

6/ Details of the critique

(a) A priori assumptions?
The opening move is to assert boldly that the philosophers have proceeded from certain "*a priori* assumptions"[36] about the forms of knowledge and that their work "appears to be based on an absolutist conception of a set of distinct forms of knowledge which correspond closely to the traditional areas of the academic curriculum and thus justify, rather than examine, what are no more than the socio-historical constructs of a particular time."[37] If this means that the philosophers have not paused to ask if there *are* distinct forms, but have merely assumed this to be the case and proceeded to delineate

them, then my opening quotation from Hirst and Peters is sufficient to show that the accusation is false. If it means on the other hand that philosophers hold to a distinction between various forms of knowledge without having or offering any reason for this view, the following quotation will reveal that the claim is wide of the mark:

> the major forms of knowledge, or disciplines, can each be distinguished by their dependence on some particular kind of test against experience for their distinctive expressions. On this ground alone however certain broad divisions are apparent. The sciences depend crucially on empirical experimental and observational tests, mathematics depends on deductive demonstrations from certain axioms.[38]

The word "absolute" also requires attention. The philosopher may claim that the distinction between empirical science and deductive mathematics is genuine, that it does not collapse, and is not arbitrary. It is *possible* to use the word "absolute" to make this point, though I am not aware that philosophers do put the matter this way. (They speak of one form not being reducible to another, of the forms being independent, or having independent character.) Unfortunately, the word "absolute" may be used to suggest that any distinctions drawn cannot be *challenged* or *questioned*. We need to be quite clear that this suggestion is not at all implied by the view that the forms are different or independent; and philosophers have admitted that "much of the work in this area is controversial."[39]

These observations show that Michael Young is attacking a straw opponent when he continues to charge that certain distinctions are "taken for granted."[40] Taking things for granted is a serious threat to open-minded inquiry; but there is no reason why a defender of the view that distinct forms of knowledge can be differentiated must take this for granted. It cannot, moreover, be inferred from the fact that A accepts an existing or traditional distinction that he has taken it for granted, i.e., failed to examine it critically. Young accuses

Hirst of failing to examine the traditional curriculum *because* his work ends by drawing distinctions which give some support to the traditional curriculum. But it must be obvious that a critical examination of an existing distinction could in the end support that distinction as genuine. As Antony Flew observes, Young "shares the too-common assumption that it is a necessary, indeed perhaps sufficient, condition of a critical approach that such an approach must result in the rejection of some established belief."[41] And, we might add, it is an equally common misconception about open-minded inquiry, as the earlier quotation from Young reveals.[42]

(b) Traditionalism?

Young's position develops into a more extreme relativism as the following remarks show. Referring to the distinction between empirical and conceptual matters, he says: "I remind you again that it is only a particular Anglo-American tradition of philosophy that takes such distinctions for granted."[43] Elsewhere he adds: "I think my difficulty is in the way you take for granted, and do not call into question, certain distinctions particularly those between necessary and contingent statements and between meaning and value.... These may be hallowed by traditional usage, but then so are many things you would not presuppose in an argument."[44]

Surely it can be no serious objection to a distinction that it is only maintained by a particular tradition. From the fact that tradition X *alone* maintains p, nothing at all follows about the truth or falsity of p. Antony Flew has acutely pointed out that when Young refers to what are "no more than the socio-historical constructs of a particular time" he has gone beyond what he is entitled to say on the evidence (i.e., that they *are* the socio-historical constructs of a particular time) and has committed the "Debunker's Fallacy."[45] A similar move may be detected in Young's reference to "only a particular Anglo-American tradition" which trades on the effect of "only" suggesting "merely."[46] This can help to discredit the distinction, when the fact that the tradition is *alone* in its view logically cannot discredit that view.

Secondly, no one concerned about open-minded inquiry would want to ignore serious voices which raise queries about traditional distinctions; and indeed the particular tradition of philosophy referred to by Young does contain disputes about the fact/value distinction, the analytic/synthetic distinction and so on. But

(i)   from the fact that objections are raised, we cannot conclude that the distinction in question is untenable. As we have seen, a distinction may survive critical scrutiny.

(ii)   from the fact that the distinction between X and Y may be blurred in places, we cannot infer that the distinction is *altogether* spurious. Mount Everest *is* more than a hill.

(iii)   from the fact that A utilizes a distinction, we cannot infer either that he believes the distinction is *always* clear, or that he ignores, or is unaware of, criticism of the distinction. He may hold that the distinction is genuine without closing, or attempting to close, the minds of his students to those who would reject the distinction.

It is no mark of open-mindedness, however, to hold the view that "all bachelors are unmarried" may not be a conceptual truth, or to hold that conceptual analysis might be able to tell us how many children of divorced parents become alcoholics, on the ground that the distinction between empirical and conceptual issues is not clear at every point. Furthermore, the distinction as such is in no way obliterated by the observation that science makes use of concepts. "We *conceptualise* our sense of the natural world and others."[47] Because an inquiry is in part empirical and in part conceptual no more shows that the distinction does not exist than the fact that a single object may have both intrinsic and extrinsic value shows that this distinction is meaningless. Similarly, the fact that a person who is a philosopher may have interesting and important things to say about science does nothing to show that these disciplines are not distinct; Young's observations on this point are therefore quite irrelevant to the central issue.[48]

(c) Ulterior motives?

Let us return to Young's comment, quoted earlier, about "the social evaluations of knowledge implicit in such curricula." To understand this, we need to look at a passage earlier in the same paper:

> The expansion of knowledge, and the access to it, is paralleled by its increasing differentiation. *Empirically* we could no doubt also demonstrate that increasing differentiation is a necessary condition for some groups to be in a position to legitimize "their knowledge" as superior or of high value. This high value is institutionalised by the creation of formal educational establishments to "transmit" it to specially selected members of the society. Thus highly-valued knowledge becomes enshrined in the academy or school and provides a standard against which all else that is known is compared.[49]

Of course, it is a logical truth that unless X is distinguished from Y, X will not be hailed as superior to Y. But

(i)   we cannot conclude that the distinction is spurious because it is put to an objectionable use (assuming for the sake of Young's argument that the use is objectionable).

(ii)   just because X is a logically necessary condition of Y, we cannot infer that without Y we would have no reason to pursue X.

(iii)   we cannot abandon the distinction just because A had a selfish motive in drawing attention to it.

If A has a personal stake in the continuing existence of departments of philosophy in universities, it may yet be that the arguments he employs are good ones in defence of the continued existence of such departments. In fact, Hirst holds that "a liberal education will be thus composed of the study of at least paradigm examples of all of the various forms of knowledge."[50] That is, the claim is not made that one form is superior to another, and the differentiation of forms does not *imply* that that one is superior to another. Contrary to

Young's argument, there is no difficulty at all in recognizing that X may be different from Y without being regarded as inferior or superior. On the other hand, of course, if we follow Young and abandon all our distinctions as purely arbitrary, it will necessarily be impossible to separate the concepts of differentiation and stratification. Young argues that the separation of these concepts is a revolutionary move in curriculum theory, to the extent that our very concepts of teacher, pupil, and examination, based (as he thinks) on a model of curriculum which distinguishes high status and low status knowledge, would become meaningless. But against this it must be said that our *concept* of teaching is not tied to a value criterion at all. A is teaching B if he is trying to get B to learn (in which case B is A's pupil) but B may be learning something valuable or trivial.

(d)   A rigid hierarchy of subjects

Young's further fears for open-minded teaching emerge when he writes:

> If knowledge is highly stratified there will be a clear distinction between what is taken to count as knowledge, and what is not, on the basis of which processes of selection and exclusion for curricula will take place. It would follow that this type of curricular organization presupposes and serves to legitimate a rigid hierarchy between teacher and taught, for if not, some access to control by the pupils would be implied and thus the processes of exclusion and selection would become open for modification and change.[51]

It is true, of course, that if we are ever to regard one form of knowledge as superior to another, we will require some criteria of knowledge in the first place. Similarly, if we are to differentiate forms of knowledge, we will need to work with a concept of knowledge. In this argument, Young holds that a stratified curriculum *presupposes* a rigid hierarchy. But this is not in fact a logically necessary condition because both teachers and students could arrive through open-minded inquiry and deliberation at curriculum decisions. The criteria of knowledge may themselves be subject to ongoing critical examination by both teachers and students and curricular arrangements and decisions may be regarded as revisable.

Young works with the empirical assumption that those in power will differentiate and stratify knowledge, and limit access to knowledge and the relations between knowledge areas, to their own advantage.[52] This is an interesting and testable hypothesis. But perhaps because he rejects the distinction between the empirical and the conceptual (notwithstanding that he *employs* the distinction himself),[53] he attempts to show that the differentiation of distinct forms of knowledge *logically* implies rigidity, lack of openness, conservatism, and elitism. That none of these features is logically implied, however, is clear when we simply realize that their denial in the context of a curriculum based on distinct forms of knowledge does not entail a contradiction. Careful attention to the forms of knowledge could reveal that many children have only been introduced at school to a limited number of forms, despite the fact that they were studying many different subjects, i.e., it might serve to *expose* elitism. Secondly, the fact that X is distinct from Y in no way forecloses discussion on the many links which may yet be found between them. Thirdly, that we think that X and Y are distinct in no way threatens open-mindedness, for we can continue to entertain objections to this claim, and we can look for instances in which the distinction is less sharp.

7/ Concluding comment

Any attempt to rule out open-mindedness because a certain subject is being taught, or because certain subjects are distinguished, is bound to fail for the reasons presented earlier in chapter 2 concerning the criterion of content. That A is learning a certain set of beliefs can neither ensure that he is becoming open-minded nor that he is becoming closed-minded. That B is teaching a certain set of beliefs cannot tell us what *attitude* he is adopting towards those beliefs. That a certain set of beliefs is liable to be biased cannot show that it is necessarily biased. That a variety of influences may be at work on us cannot show that we have no ability to reflect critically on our preferences in the arts. Holding that a distinction is *genuine* (i.e., having a particular belief) does not show that the belief is held dogmatically.

Since, however, open-mindedness is related to the *way* in which we hold our beliefs, or, in the case of teaching, to the way in which we present, or deal with, beliefs, it is clearly necessary to inquire further into *methods* of teaching. In chapter 4 we have already paid attention to the claim that in the area of controversial issues the teacher must adopt the method of neutral chairmanship if he or she is to be open-minded. In turning now to look at general methods such as lecturing and discussion, it will also be necessary to separate conceptual and empirical issues. Are some methods *in principle* at odds, or in accord, with open-mindedness? Or is it that some general methods tend *in fact* to promote open-mindedness more readily than others? A clear answer to the second question is often hard to establish simply because the two issues are not kept distinct, and *a priori* claims are often misleadingly presented as plain matters of fact.

Open-mindedness and teaching methods

6

1/ Unexamined assumptions

One cannot tell in advance of experience whether or not a particular teaching technique or method will be successful, i.e., will eventuate in the student learning. As Stenhouse has recently observed, "the development of teaching strategies can never be *a priori*."[1] And we are only now beginning to appreciate how complex such empirical inquiries are. Numerous factors including the size, acoustics, illumination, and ventilation of the classroom need to be taken into consideration as well as a host of psychological factors.[2] One peculiar difficulty centres on the attitude which the student has to the method being used. If a student *expects* a lecture, for example, to be a period of "information input" and nothing more, this very expectation may serve to prevent the student from thinking for himself.[3] Thus, in this sort of case, we cannot be confident that if a claim is false (e.g., the claim that method X cannot teach attitude Y), then experience will eventually show that it is false; for the false belief may serve to prevent attitude Y being learned via this method. The prophecy is fulfilled. We need to compare the results of student groups who believe that method X is poor, with those who have no such belief. Thus a lack of open-mindedness about the method on the part of the students may serve to make the method ineffective.

There is, however, some reason to believe that certain methods are regarded as ineffective in the absence of firm evidence. As recently as 1971, Bligh concluded that "we know little of scientific value" about lecturing,[4] for example, and Wallen and Travers speak of "little direct evidence" with respect to the comparative merits of lecturing and discussion in connection with problem-solving and application of knowledge.[5] But this latter reference provides an interesting case of the way in which assumptions and prejudices can creep into empirical research. In view of the evidence which the authors themselves cite, it is frankly amazing that they should assert confidently that "although some learning takes place by this procedure, the lecture method is a rather inefficient method of producing learning."[6] The available evidence simply does not warrant this assertion, and as Bligh notes "the strength with which opinions are held is frequently greater than the strength of their grounds."[7]

Despite Stenhouse's professed commitment to empirical investigation, there is, in fact, clear evidence that he engages in just the sort of *a priori* legislation about methods which he himself condemns. In his paper on "Open-minded Teaching"[8] he comes out against what he calls "formal instruction," but provides no empirical evidence in support of his view, though he explains that "the project is therefore committed to responsibility (the acceptance of one's own accountability) rather than to authority (depending for justification on others)."[9] Clearly there are a number of assumptions about formal instruction which need to be examined here.

Even analytically-minded philosophers of education like Paul Hirst and Richard Peters do not entirely escape the phenomenon of the unexamined assumption about certain methods. Certainly no one has better exposed the prejudice involved in thinking that a certain method *must* be ineffective than Peters himself.[10] But in his joint work with Hirst we find the remarks "teaching, and not just lecturing"[11] and "just being lectured at.'"[12] In each of these cases, they are attributing a criticism to another person; but in the discussion of the criticisms, they fail to ask if the assumptions involved are warranted.

2/ Lecturing and Listening

I will now attempt to uncover some of the unexamined assumptions which lie behind both popular and scholarly opinion about lecturing and listening which help to explain why it is so commonly believed, in the absence of hard evidence, that when lecturing is occurring (and consequently when, in the normal situation, students are listening) open-mindedness is lost. When these assumptions are shown to be without foundation, it will appear that there is no reason *in principle* to associate closed-mindedness with formal instruction. It will then be possible to return with a clear mind to whatever empirical evidence is available. I will in effect be attempting to isolate those thoughts which have led people to condemn this approach to teaching *a priori*, and will thus be concerned, in an appropriate way for a philosopher, with a person's motives.[13]

(a) The analogy with preaching
Something of this suggestion is associated with the second of the two comments by Hirst and Peters about "just being lectured at."[14] It comes out explicitly in certain educational reports,[15] and explains why it is believed by such writers that there is something madly paradoxical in the idea of a lecture being given on the topic of discussion methods of teaching. Such instructors, it is urged, do not practise what they *preach*, and the word chosen is significant.[16] It seems to be assumed that a lecturer is necessarily supporting a particular position, and that his audience are expected to accept his views because he is the authority.

Neither of these beliefs is implied in the idea of a lecture. Though the point is not well understood, a lecturer in university or school is not necessarily advocating a particular belief or practice at all. The lecture may simply explore the arguments for and against, and the evidence relevant to, a particular issue. Thus the notion of a lecture on the merits of discussion methods of teaching is perfectly coherent. And the lecturer need not expect his audience to accept his views, when he does defend a position, on authority. The classical Greek term διάλεξις was essentially connected with ideas of reason-giving and argument, and these remain part of the connotation of the term "lecture" when it refers to a teaching method.

Of course, those who have had access to a pulpit or podium have often seized the opportunity to browbeat their audience into meek submission. And an important ambiguity has developed in the English term "lecture," which does not exist in all modern languages, and which can serve to discredit the lecture as a method of *teaching*. Consider a recent report on the Nova Scotia legislature which appeared in a Canadian newspaper under the heading "Speaker lectures members." The report tells the reader that the members of the house were cautioned to follow the rules during the question period. (We may infer that some infringements of the rules of the house had been occurring.) There is the suggestion in this context of a reprimand or formal reproof. The informal analogue of this is the sort of case in which a parent "lectures" his child and, as we say, "lays down the law." What has happened is that, because reprimands have often been delivered in lengthy, formal, and detailed addresses, i.e., lectures, the concept of lecture has in some contexts come to acquire the meaning of reprimand or reproof, and dictionaries in fact list this as one of the meanings of the term.

There are, as we would expect, some similarities between this use of lecture and that in which it refers to a teaching method. Both normally involve some authority-figure addressing a silent audience in fairly formal and lengthy fashion. But important differences remain. The Speaker in the legislature example or the parent are saying what the rules are, or will be. They are not normally involved in deploying arguments to defend such rules. Those being lectured know the rules, otherwise a reprimand would be inappropriate, and have been falling short of the conduct demanded of them. The primary purpose of this "lecture" is not to teach people what the rules are, nor is it to justify them, but rather to demand obedience and conformity. It is not an open-minded consideration of the rules, but a demand that the rules be obeyed. The rules are not open for discussion; they are to be followed.

It is not difficult to see how these connotations of the reprimand use of "lecturing" could have contributed to the view that the lecture method of teaching is at odds with open-minded teaching. To avoid this we need to recall that in lecturing, the teacher need not be *authoritarian* and assert that certain beliefs *must* be accepted. The lecture method of teaching is not inconsistent with the criteria of educational activities, i.e., a worthwhile issue can be pursued in a rational and critical manner, with respect for the autonomy and integrity of the audience. Lecturers *may* engage in propaganda, indoctrination, evangelizing, and haranguing—but there is no reason why these should be thought to be necessarily associated with formal instruction.

(b) The charge of passivity
It may be insisted, however, that even if we eliminate the reprimand sense and the connotations of preaching, there remains in the lecture method a fatal obstacle to open-minded inquiry. While the lecturer is lecturing, the audience is silent and *passive*. For example, two recent researchers note that psychologists believe that *activity* on the part of the learner is an important principle in learning and they add: "It is relevant here that one of the main criticisms of the lecture by medical students is that it is a passive method of learning. (British Medical Students Association, 1965)."[17] It is then a short step from the introduction of the notion of passivity to the view that during the lecture students are not being critical, not questioning, and indeed have closed minds. Thus we find it said of the classroom lecture that

the teacher becomes a "deity at the podium" dispensing neatly packaged units of information to captive students.... In such an atmosphere, the pupil often comes to regard information as a set of "givens" — a series of facts or solutions not open to dispute.... It is often easier for the learner to agree with what is said than to dispute its merit: how easy is it, for example, for a student to challenge a professor's opinion before 150 students during a 50-minute lecture?[18]

Admittedly, the word "often" here reveals that empirical claims are being made; but my immediate concern is to show how conceptual confusion can distort such empirical investigation. For example, it is surely a confusion to equate "challenging an opinion" with the overt statement of disagreement in public. Empirical investigation might reveal that a certain percentage of students will not express disagreement in public with the lecturer even when encouraged to do so. But this, of course, does not show that these students *agree* with what has been said, nor that they are failing to challenge the professor's opinions.

It is, of course, similarly absurd to move from talk of physical passivity to claims about mental passivity, notwithstanding that the slide is frequently made. (There are as many now who believe that a silent classroom is necessarily bad as once believed it to be necessarily good.)[19] Even a writer like Hyman, who sets out a defence of lecturing, couches the defence in terms which undermine the value of listening.[20] He argues that in a lecture students may be actively involved, but this turns out to depend on whether or not they are asked questions to which they are expected to respond.

The model is the familiar one of a receptacle being topped up with information. Something is being done to the student. He is a passive recipient and, the implication is clear, uncritical. For example, it has recently been suggested that "if the teacher wants the students to reflect on and confront their attitudes, the discussion method may be more effective than the more passive learning environment of the lecture."[21] But because a student is sitting still and is thus passive, no implication at all follows about his thought processes. We need to test this suggestion empirically, with a clear mind about the ambiguity of passivity. The danger is that the ambiguity can lead us to think that an empirical test is not necessary. It may be, of course, that a good deal of listening is *in fact* quite uncritical, but there is no reason why it must be so. We do have the concept of critical listening, and this may lead to the acceptance or rejection of the ideas in question. The student who is silent, note-taking, etc., may be actively reflecting on the points being made, thinking up objections and criticisms.

(c) Conviction and conformity
Certain expressions in English can also foster the mistaken view that since the lecture method places the students in the role of listeners, it threatens open-mindedness by emphasizing conviction and conformity. Consider the following cases: (i) "You've got to listen to me"—a suspect to sceptical police officers; (ii) "My children will not listen to me"—perennial complaint of parents. In the first of these cases, the suspect actually wants the police to *believe* what he is saying. In the second, the parent bemoans the fact that his children do not *obey* him. These are quite normal uses of the word "listening" in ordinary talk. Clearly, however, if we start to think of the meaning of listening in terms of belief and obedience, we raise some serious difficulties in the context of education. The indoctrinated person has conviction and conforms to the wishes of the party or church; but it is his conviction and conformity which lead others to deny that he has the outlook of the educated person. The point is not that conformity and belief are necessarily at odds with becoming educated.[22] But the cases of listening cited above do not allow for rejection of ideas, advice, pleas, etc., which clearly must be allowed for in education and in open-minded inquiry.

I suggest, however, that in the two cases above the concept of listening is used *figuratively*. The police officers and the children may listen patiently and carefully and yet "fail to listen" in the ways suggested, i.e., they did not believe what they were told, and they did not obey the order. These cases reflect the speaker's view of the obvious truth of what he is saying. *If only* the other person would just listen (literally), he could not help but believe or obey. So strong is this feeling, that when conformity and/or belief is not forthcoming, the person concludes that the other person could not have listened. The fact is, of course, that even if my claims are correct or my advice sound, another person may well listen to what I say but ultimately disagree.[23]

We need to insist that the officers and the children may *listen* to, and not merely hear, what is said. To listen is to attend to what is heard (listening *to*) or to what may be heard (listening *for*); it is to concentrate on aural perception. The officers and children may pay full and careful attention and yet reject the plea or the advice. And the rejection *per se* does not show that their minds were closed. In the police/suspect case, the figure of speech is litotes. We say that we *only* want the officers to listen, but we really want them to believe, hence it is an understatement. In the parent/child case, the figure is hyperbole, for we exaggerate what the child will not do. In characterizing such uses as figurative, however, I do not wish to imply that such uses may not have had a profound effect upon the attitude to listening (and hence to lecturing) in the educational context. Indeed, in a tradition of schooling which emphasized literal listening in order to achieve conviction and conformity, one can readily imagine how confusion might arise. The point of making clear the distinction between the literal and the figurative is to bring out the fact that objections which may be legitimate in one context cannot be assumed to hold in another. Literal listening in itself constitutes no threat to open-minded inquiry.[24]

(d)   Ignoring the students
It is commonly alleged that lecturing clashes with open inquiry because the teacher does not attend to the viewpoints of the students: "Teaching is a matter of identifying individual weaknesses and correcting them. Lecturing is talking, teaching is listening. It is impossible to listen to a group of a

hundred."[25] Perhaps we can interpret this as a rhetorical way of making the point that if one is going to aim at a person learning something, we will need to attend to his efforts in order to see if our strategy is working.[26] And if our teaching is to be open-minded, we will need to attend to what the learner has to say in case our position may be faulty. To these criticisms we can reply as follows:

(i)   A defence of the lecture method does not entail a commitment to the lecture system in which lecturing is the only method of teaching employed.[27] Lecturing can be combined with other methods.

(ii)   Even if lecturing is the only method used, it does not follow that open-mindedness is lost for the teacher can raise objections to, and difficulties in, his own position, and discover in other ways the criticisms the students would raise. He must "listen" to his students, but we cannot insist that he must attend aurally to their criticisms, for this would be to select *one* possible means of discovering their criticisms and to make it the *only* possible means. He must attend in some way to their criticisms, but he could do this, for example, by reading papers written by the students.

When we learn that A is lecturing, we do not thereby learn whether or not his teaching is open-minded. We could only do this by looking at the way in which he lectures. However, empirical research might discover how effective this particular method is with respect to maintaining or promoting open-mindedness. The research findings in fact indicate:

(i)   "Lectures are as effective as other methods for teaching information, but not more so"[28] and that "with respect to immediate mastery of factual information, most studies find no significant differences between lecture and discussion methods."[29] I have not encountered any evidence which shows that the students *hold* the beliefs gained through a lecture in a closed-minded way.

(ii)   Studies do seem to suggest that discussion methods are more effective than lectures with respect to changing attitudes[30] (though the number of studies here is much smaller; and nearly all originate in the United States, which raises problems about the possible influence of cultural factors.)

It may be then that discussions would be more useful than lectures, if our aim in teaching is to *develop* more open-minded attitudes in students who are somewhat closed-minded. I have not found any evidence which suggests that lectures might promote closed-mindedness in students who are relatively open-minded. If, however, in view of the fact that present research suggests that discussions might be more effective in *changing* attitudes, we decide to restrict lecturing, it should be remembered that this is done on empirical grounds. We should not close our minds to the possibility that the causes of the relative ineffectiveness of lectures might be eliminated. We do close our minds to this if we adopt the *a priori* approach criticized earlier.

Studies which show that attitudes cannot be established or changed simply by giving the student verbal information, cannot be cited as evidence for the ineffectiveness of *lectures* in establishing or maintaining the attitude of open-mindedness or any other attitude. For while it is clear that telling children (by rational argument or emotional appeal) to be open-minded may be useless, it does not follow that the manifestation of open-mindedness by the lecturer will be ineffective. Yet it is commonly thought that the ineffectiveness of "telling" is a sufficient condemnation of the lecture in this connection.

3/ Discussion and open-mindedness

In the case of lecturing, we saw that certain *a priori* reasons were offered why this method could not be open-minded, and thus careful empirical research was often thought to be unnecessary. In the area of discussion methods a reverse form of this error is encountered, for conceptual reasons are blown up into procedural principles in the belief that discussion *must* foster open-mindedness.

I will argue that the *concept* of discussion is logically related to the idea of open-mindedness. It must be admitted, however, that if we survey *all* the ways in which the word "discussion" is employed in English, we will find that it is sometimes used in contexts in which a closed mind is aimed at. Consider, for example, the following report of a practice which the participants describe as a discussion:

> All members of the congregation have studied the article in question during the previous week. Whoever leads the discussion takes the week's article paragraph by paragraph. He asks the questions set; the answers have all been underlined during the week, and there is some competition among the congregation as to who can get his hand up quickest and catch the leader's eye most often. ... At no time during any of the meetings – and least of all during the Watchtower Discussion – did any participant question any of the printed conclusions or opinions.[31]

The writer introduces these comments with the remark that "it all depends what you call a discussion. If your idea of a discussion is an occasion when different views on a subject are aired and compared, then the Watchtower Discussion is not for you."[32] This, however, misses the point; for we are not concerned whether or not we are for or against such meetings – this is surely a matter for private judgment – but rather with whether or not such meetings are *appropriately* called "discussions." It is overly casual to say that "it all depends what you call a discussion," as if nothing turned on this. And indeed this writer elsewhere in the paper uses the term "discussion," without hesitation or scare quotes, to refer to the door-step preaching which characterizes this movement.

The important point is that the practices described above *violate* the criteria of discussion which hold in other and ordinary contexts:

(a)   If A is prepared to discuss his position, it is implied that he is prepared to examine his position critically and rationally. It does not simply mean that he is prepared to *state* his reasons, for two sides can state their reasons in what is no more than an exchange of ideologies. The dogmatist is often prepared to *state* his reasons but is not prepared to reflect on them in the light of the objections raised. If one is seriously taking part in a discussion, one must listen to the criticisms of others and attempt to meet them at the level of rational inquiry. This does not mean simply rehearsing previously worked-out defences.

(b)   If the answer to a question is a plain matter of fact, there may be nothing to discuss. We simply look up the answer in a suitable place. If different answers are suggested in the absence of the authoritative source, it may be possible to show that some of them cannot be correct, or that one is correct, and thus discussion enters in. But in the Watchtower case, there is both an authoritative source *and* an absence of differing viewpoints, hence there is nothing to discuss. "A disquisition in which a subject is treated from different sides" (*Shorter Oxford English Dictionary*) is an accurate description of a discussion as the concept operates outside certain specialized and technical contexts (such as the religious group above).

(c)   Even when an individual alone *discusses* a problem (in a book, in an examination, etc.), the plural aspect is retained, for it is implied that he will consider various positions which might be, or which have been, taken on the issue in question. But this attention to a variety of viewpoints is absent in the above case.

In view of these points then, it is not at all an arbitrary piece of verbal legislation to balk at the application of the term "discussion" in the above case, for the standard implications of the concept will not be met. The very distinction between open- and closed-minded inquiry, which the word "discussion" serves to underline, is obliterated, and discussion is confused with indoctrination. If the distinction between open-mindedness and closed-mindedness is important and worth preserving, it cannot be a matter of indifference if the word "discussion" is used in a way which can only undermine the distinction. Nor can it be said that the term has now come to include new practices (in the way that a library now stocks records as well as books), because as we have seen the essential features of discussion in the ordinary sense and the religious "discussion" are incompatible.

One lesson we can draw from this is that although discussion and open-mindedness are *conceptually* linked, not everything *called* a discussion will manifest open-mindedness. Researchers report, for example, that teachers will sometimes *call* a particular class a discussion lesson, even though they have actively discouraged interaction between the students, fearing disorder.[33]

4/ Discussion and the fostering of open-mindedness

(a) Reflection

As a result perhaps of the fact that "research findings are somewhat equivocal concerning the relative effectiveness of lecture and discussion in inducing attitude change,"[34] we find in fact a good deal of *speculation* about the empirical connection. Moreover, the supporters of discussion methods often confuse conceptual and empirical matters. Thus, if A is seriously taking part in a discussion, he will be reflecting critically on his own views; but it does not of course follow that students will *in fact* think in this way. It has been claimed, however, that "if the student is asked by another student or the teacher to state an opinion on an issue, he is compelled to reflect whether he indeed has an opinion, and if so, what that opinion is."[35] This is surely false. The student may refuse to say anything. He may simply produce a statement which he has not reflected on at all. This claim has confused what would be occurring if the student were involved in a discussion, with what may actually be occurring.

(b) Coercion

Discussion is, of course, *conceptually* at odds with coercion. If a conclusion is forced, predetermined, or coerced, the notion of discussion has been lost, for the conclusion is brought about not by rational argument but by pressure.[36] This, of course, does not rule out arguing powerfully for a certain conclusion, but it must be *argument*. In schools, however, it is often the case that "the student simply may be coerced by another student or faction of students to change his expressed opinions, especially where the student holds an opinion considered deviant."[37] It is important to realize that even though the other students are trying to argue rationally for their position, our coerced student may perceive a threat where none exists, or may fear being alone in his opinions, and thus give up his view for no good reason. He may hold the new view in a closed-minded way, in order to be considered a good member of the group. Thus a discussion does not guarantee an open-minded outcome.

Research shows that minority opinions in a discussion are often protected in a group which has a leader, but in leaderless groups they are often abandoned. Beard and Bligh comment that "this suggests that free group discussion with an observer may be more effective in encouraging critical thinking than discussion in a group with a teacher."[38] They merely put this forward as a suggestion, but it is clear that any further test in this area would need to ask why the minority abandons its position. If they have merely been coerced, they do not display critical thinking, even if the view they come to adopt is the correct one.

(c) Irrationality
It is also possible for discussions to be so arranged or structured that a belief may be irrationally induced or reinforced.[39] Suppose that a teacher gets a class to discuss with him which is the best way to worship God. Participating in this discussion may reinforce or induce the belief that there *is* a God, and that there is some way of worshipping Him which is better than others. The discussion does not raise the questions, "Does God exist?" or "Should God be worshipped?" If we were to come in on such a discussion lesson midway, we could not be sure that these prior questions had been considered, and we

might not recognize a subtle case of indoctrination. As far as the specific issue is concerned, it might be a very open-minded inquiry. At the same time, it could be serving the purposes of the dogmatist.

Of course, if a student raises the prior questions, the concept of discussion will be violated if his questions are legislated out of order. This teacher would be no more a champion of discussion than a person would be a supporter of freedom of worship who limited the choice to different faiths within the realm of Christianity. Still, the indoctrinator is hoping that the questions being begged will not be raised, and it cannot be asserted that the class do not discuss the question "Which is the best way to worship God?" They do discuss *this*, but they do not recognize the limits which have been imposed on the discussion. Once again, a discussion does not ensure open-mindedness.

(d)   A contrast with lecturing?

It is worth noting that any attempt to support the discussion *method* because of conceptual links with open-mindedness would in any case also help to support the lecture method. This is simply because a lecture may itself be, or involve, a discussion of an issue. Thus all the overtones of open-mindedness would apply equally to a lecture conducted in a certain way.

(e)   Authority

Although the *concept* of discussion is not violated if the teacher in the group defends a position with argument and evidence, it is quite possible that some of the students will be swayed not by the argument or the evidence, but by the status of the teacher as authority-figure. This is not, of course, to endorse Stenhouse's view that "the authority position of the teacher is much stronger than most teachers realize, and that it is almost insuperably difficult for him to put forward his own points of view without implying that controversial issues can be settled on the basis of the authority of others."[40] We simply need to remember that it *may* happen and not to hold that it is almost *bound* to happen.[41] I have not, in fact, found any evidence which shows that it is "insuperably difficult" to escape the implication that in expressing his opinion a teacher indicates or suggests that controversial issues can be settled on the basis of authority.[42] In stating this view so strongly and confidently, there is the danger that it will be accepted as obviously correct, and thus research is felt to be superfluous. Similarly there will be no investigation of the ways in which a teacher might seek to counteract any such effect.

(f)   Hidden curriculum effect

It may be reasonably maintained that insofar as the educated person is also open-minded (as was argued in chapter 3), it follows that the views of an educated person are open for discussion. (Qualifications would have to be entered here, with respect to a person who might be afraid to discuss his views, or who might feel entitled to remain silent about certain private and personal matters, etc.) But it cannot be assumed that the discussion method of teaching will inevitably lead to the development of a willingness to discuss on the part of those who are taught in this way. Much depends upon the way in which the discussions are conducted. Students might, for example, be silently resolving to keep their views to themselves rather than be exposed to hostile reactions. As we have been recently reminded, there is often a "hidden curriculum" at work.[43]

(g)   Open expression

We should also guard against the fallacy of thinking that if A is becoming willing to express his views *openly*, he is thereby becoming willing to think in an open-minded way. A view which is only expressed is not necessarily representative of an open mind, for some people are quite prepared to reveal their prejudices publicly.

(h)   Brainstorming

Studies have also investigated the use of a "brainstorming" technique in which students are asked to supply as many solutions to a given problem as they can think up in a speci-fied time period, *without pausing to evaluate the suggestions criti-cally*. It appears that this technique *in fact* produces more creative, useful, and original solutions than having the stu-dents record only those suggestions which they *think* are cre-ative, etc.[44] It might be tempting initially to draw some conclusions from this about the degree of open-mindedness involved, perhaps following Dewey's analysis of open-mind-edness as "accessibility of mind to any and every considera-tion that will throw light upon the situation;"[45] and some recent writers *have* introduced the idea of open-mindedness in commenting on the possibilities of this technique.[46] The ob-jection to this line of thought, however, is simply that the pro-duction of a greater number of suggested solutions (which have not been critically assessed) can tell us neither that the students were on this occasion willing to revise or abandon the solution they would personally opt for, nor that partici-pating in such an exercise contributed to the development of such a *trait* of intellect. These hypotheses would have to be tested independently. They cannot be logically inferred from the data. It is not impossible that a student who actually pro-duces in the above manner a solution which is at once both creative and correct, could refuse to accept it as the solution when the time for critical evaluation comes.

5/ A general comment on the research concerning lectures and discussion groups

I have tried to show that ambiguity, figurative language, con-ceptual confusion, and *a priori* assumptions can persuade us to condemn an approach as being necessarily at odds with open-mindedness, in which case we cease to look for ways in which practical deficiencies might be remedied. Conversely, we can be led to embrace a method of teaching in the belief that it is certain to foster open-mindedness, in which case we fail to ask if it is *actually* doing so. Even when empirical work is undertaken, it is extremely easy to misinterpret the signifi-cance of the results if we do not retain a clear concept of open-mindedness. (Consider, for example, the earlier discussion of "passivity" and "brainstorming.")

It would be a complete misunderstanding of my position to suggest that *all* we need is conceptual clarity. My claim is that this is necessary, not that it is sufficient. We also need empirical evidence, or we will not know how to avoid methods which conflict with our ideal. Consider, for example, the case of a teacher who wishes to present two conflicting views on an issue without supporting either one. That is, he wishes to leave it up to the students which, if any, side they will support. In this case, he has decided to be neutral and wishes to be open-minded. He wants to succeed in being as impartial and objective in his presentation as possible. The situation is complicated as follows: he will need one lecture-hour to present position A properly, and a second hour one week later to present position B. Suppose he wonders at this point if the outcome will be influenced by the fact that A is presented first and B second. The only way to answer this, of course, is to test the hypothesis. In fact, studies suggest that if two sides are presented a week apart, the one more recently presented tends to be viewed as more convincing. If the two sides are presented in the same hour, the *first* presented tends to be viewed as more convincing.[47] The relevance of this data is quite simply that the teacher who is unaware of these findings may unwittingly undermine his own efforts to be open-minded. Of course, we would not convict a teacher of lacking open-mindedness because he unwittingly supported one side in this way, any more than we would condemn a teacher who is unconsciously biased as having a closed mind. But if A wishes to be an open-minded teacher, he will look for such pitfalls and attempt to avoid them.

Attention was drawn, in the preface to this book, to a growing sense of discontent with the overall research findings on teaching effectiveness. Some writers have come close indeed to a rather pessimistic view of the possibility of improving the situation. Nuthall and Snook, for example, in a thoughtful analysis of contemporary models of teaching[48] and careful survey of research findings, suggest that rational assessment in this area is well-nigh impossible: "No matter how impeccable the research designs, nor how sophisticated the statistical analysis, the research remains, for the most part, tied to the models. ... When the model loses its persuasive power it is likely to disappear from view, taking with it the research it generated."[49] The implication is clear. A model, or research based on it, is not *refuted*. It disappears as its proponents disappear from the scene.

Although I too have pointed out that, in many instances, the research findings are unclear, ambiguous, doubtful, and equivocal, I have not embraced the pessimistic view of Nuthall and Snook as reflected in the above passage. It might, therefore, be useful to look at the reasons which seem to have led these writers to the conclusion that meaningful research in this area may not be possible.

It is of great interest in the present context to note that doubts about the possibility of useful research is generated by considerations which are taken to suggest that *open-minded inquiry* is not to be found here. Thus Nuthall and Snook observe:

> Proponents of the discovery-learning model attempt to provide empirical evidence that discovery methods are better than expository methods. The important quality of this research and argument is that it is intended primarily to *persuade* the educational community. It is prejudiced research because those who undertake it delineate not only the view of teaching which they favour, but also the alternative traditional method of teaching which they are against.[50]

There is a very common fallacy at work here, one which presents itself quite blatantly in much educational commentary.[51] The accuracy and significance of research cannot be called into question by appealing to some characteristic of the person who conducted the research. The soundness of evidence is logically unrelated to, and assessed independently of, any reference to the special circumstances of the person offering it. To do otherwise is to commit the *ad hominem* fallacy.[52]

Attempts to persuade *may* be merely rhetorical, but on the other hand *rational* persuasion is also possible. We cannot question an argument on the grounds that its author wishes to persuade us of its truth or validity. We need to examine the logic of the argument and the evidence for the premises. Furthermore, as was argued in chapter 2,[53] the fact that a person believes in the truth of the hypothesis which he is setting out to examine, does not imply that the research is prejudiced in any sense which rules out rational, open-minded inquiry. We can say that the researcher is "prejudiced," if we merely mean by this that he favours a particular hypothesis; but this sense of "prejudiced" is distinct from, and does not imply, that sense which suggests "closed-minded." Similarly, we cannot conclude that the research is "contaminated" and insignificant. Again, as we saw earlier, there may well be a danger in such circumstances of bias entering in, but a danger is not yet a certainty.[54] There are no shortcuts here. We simply have to look at the merits of the argument and evidence in any given case.

Nuthall and Snook also appear to subscribe to the view that rational assessment of the *models* of teaching is not possible:

> the outcomes of this research have not affected the status of the models themselves. No one has asked the question, which of the three models is the correct model. ... By virtue of adopting one model in preference to another, those involved in the research make it impossible for agreement to be reached on what evidence would be relevant to answering such a question.[55]

And in case this should appear to be merely a sin of *omission*, they add:

> the major models of teaching operate as models in that they define how teaching should be viewed. And, in this definition, they stipulate not only what is good teaching, but also what is bad teaching or what should not be considered teaching at all. It is for this reason that the research generated by a particular model is not generally useful outside the context of that model.[56]

We may agree, I believe, with Nuthall and Snook that if a researcher is, for example, interested in the question whether or not delay in reinforcement has an effect on the learning of responses in the classroom, the results of such a study are not likely to lead anyone to abandon a behaviour-control model of teaching. On the other hand, if someone is initially attracted to a particular model, empirical evidence that such and such learning tends to be promoted by that model could lead to the model being given up. Just as we may discover unsuspected and undesirable effects of an initially attractive new drug, so too we may discover important shortcomings in an approach to teaching. Contrary indeed to the suggestion in the previous quotation but one, Nuthall and Snook themselves cite examples of how such shortcomings have led to rational reconsideration.[57]

We need, too, to be careful how we understand the term "adopt" in the context of "adopting one model in preference to another." To adopt a model in order to engage in research designed to test the effectiveness of that model is not to close our minds to the possibility that the research might bring out difficulties inherent in the model. It is not, therefore, to commit ourselves to that model in any sense which might suggest that future abandonment of the model is ruled out.[58]

If "adopt" is then understood as taking a model seriously enough to allow it to generate research, there is no reason *in principle* why we cannot return with our evidence to reconsider the model. We discover, for example, that teaching in a certain way leads to students developing rigid attitudes with respect to that which is learned. We may then ask whether or not a model which leads to such an outcome is consistent with our notion of what it means to be an educated person. If, as we argued in chapter 3, there is an inconsistency here, then we have unearthed a major defect in the model, considered as a model of teaching which is alleged to serve the aims of education.

I conclude, therefore, that we have been given no good reason to despair of open-minded inquiry in this area, notwithstanding that the research problems are very great indeed.

The systematic and rigorous gathering of evidence, however, must go hand in hand with the most careful scrutiny of the central educational concepts. It is utterly futile to rest content with the circular statement that open-mindedness is what a scale for open-mindedness measures. We need to know whether the research operates with a clear and acceptable concept of open-mindedness, whether the scale does indeed test for this attitude, and whether this is an attitude which education should promote.

6/ Independent study

It will perhaps be surprising to find a section on independent study in a chapter on teaching methods, for if a student is working independently, he is precisely *not* a pupil, i.e., he has no teacher. Normally, however, educational theorists speak of independent study as part of an overall program of teaching and learning; and the student consults his teachers who guide and encourage his efforts. Thus it is possible to view this as a form of teaching.

(a) Independent-minded

Again there are conceptual traps for the unwary. As we noted in chapter 1, an individual is independent-minded if he tends to make up his own mind. Thus, insofar as an open-minded person makes up his own mind, not on the basis of authority but on the strength of the evidence or argument, being independent-minded is a necessary condition of being open-minded. (The notions are not, however, equivalent because the independent-minded person could make up his mind in an open-minded way and then be unwilling to revise his view. I think that this unwillingness would not show that he was not independent-minded, but it would show that he was not open-minded.)

Thus independence of mind emerges as a necessary condition of open-mindedness and is therefore an important goal of education. But consider this recent observation: "In fact, it would seem that it is not the central aim of by any means all teachers; for if it were so, courses and methods of assessment would give additional credit to the capacity for independent study and thinking."[59] Insofar as this involves the comment that educational systems which claim to value independence of mind should somehow attempt to assess this in the evaluation of students, there can be no disagreement. A crucial fallacy, however, enters in, inasmuch as it is argued that independent *thinking* presupposes independent *study*, for here we find "independent" being employed in rather different ways. An individual is independent-minded if he tends to make up his own mind without relying on others. But an individual is working independently if he is working on his own, not related to others. A person is not lacking independence of mind simply because he collaborates with others, or because he is receiving instruction. The important question is whether or not he is able to *make his own decision* what to believe. It is true, as Beard says, that "methods of study should be made more effective,"[60] but it is an empirical matter to determine whether or not independent study tends to foster independent-mindedness. It is not a logical truth, for there is no contradiction at all in the idea of a person who studies on his own coming eventually under the sway of some ideology or individual. How far this happens cannot be answered from the armchair.

(b)   The concept of study
Secondly, the notion of study itself may be thought to suggest that an open-minded inquiry is necessarily occurring. The concept of study surely suggests a *careful* inquiry. A book entitled "A study of X" (or "A study in X") leads one to expect a detailed and rigorous examination of the topic in question. To study an art object, a scene, a face, an argument, a problem, etc., is to give very careful attention to the details present.

There is also a connection with an appeal to reason. To study something is to be concerned to understand or appreciate it. A person who spends a great deal of time practising basketball is not thereby said to be studying the game; but study becomes the appropriate term when the player is involved in reflection on strategy, the opposition, weaknesses in his play, and so on. "A studied look" is the face of a man pondering, weighing alternatives—in brief, engaged in thought. And we can study not only existing theories; our study may be concerned with the development of new ideas.

Yet study need not imply open-mindedness, for we have to ask what are the motives of the man engaged in thought. Is he giving careful attention to the claims of his opponents in order to show that they must be mistaken? Rival political groups often compete for space in the correspondence columns of our papers, and they could not "demolish" each other's views if they did not study those views. But it is an undeniable fact that the attitude of open-mindedness rarely comes through in such exchanges.

It is true that study entails the careful and thoughtful examination of arguments and beliefs, but this cannot guarantee that a person who studies will not end by holding the beliefs he has studied as a dead dogma.[61] Thus we cannot infer from the fact that a person is studying that he is engaged in an activity which will promote open-mindedness in him.

7/ Concluding comment

Reflection on the *idea* of a lecture, a discussion, or independent study—or indeed on any method of study—cannot in itself tell us which methods to avoid or which to embrace if we are to foster open-mindedness in our students. Conceptual analysis does show that the notion of formal instruction is not in itself incompatible with open-minded teaching. Similarly, analysis shows that non-neutrality on the part of a teacher in a discussion does not in itself rule out open-minded teaching. A teacher may manifest a closed mind in a lecture, in discussion, or in his capacity as resource person in an independent study program. If he is to know which strategies tend to promote open-mindedness in others, he must turn to the available evidence. If he does not take care to avoid strategies which conflict with his expressed aim, he will not be regarded as being in serious pursuit of that aim. But unless he operates with a clear concept of open-mindedness, he is in danger of misinterpreting the available evidence, much of which is presently stated in misleading terms by empirical researchers who themselves lack a clear concept.

Objections to open-mindedness in teaching

7

1/ The major arguments of this book so far can be summarized in the following six points:

(a) Open-mindedness is logically unrelated to *what* one believes: neutrality and doubt are neither necessary nor sufficient for open-mindedness.

(b) Open-mindedness *is* logically related to the concept of education and is consistent with other valuable attitudes.

(c) Open-mindedness is an attitude we can have to settled as well as to ongoing issues. It involves being willing to revise one's views in the light of counter-evidence. No subject matter in itself clashes with open-mindedness.

(d) No particular method of teaching in itself excludes or ensures open-minded teaching.

(e) There is some evidence that discussion methods may be more effective in changing attitudes than more formal approaches, but the evidence relating to the claim that the neutral-chairman approach more effectively promotes open-mindedness than other approaches is inconclusive.

(f) There is much evidence available indicating the many ways in which a teacher may unwittingly fall short of objectivity and impartiality, and anyone seriously pursuing open-mindedness cannot ignore this evidence.

Imagine then that a teacher, persuaded by the above arguments, plans to manifest in his or her teaching the attitude of being willing to revise one's beliefs in the light of decisive counter-evidence or argument, and to manifest this in a method or combination of methods which, in the light of the available evidence, seems most likely to promote the same attitude in the students. If such a person genuinely has an open-minded outlook, there remains one serious hurdle before his plan can be implemented. There are, in fact, many voices opposed to open-mindedness in education and it is necessary that such objections as exist be examined before we can proceed with a clear conscience.

2/ The open consideration of issues

Contemporary educational theorists who are opposed to indoctrination, propaganda, bias, dogmatic instruction, and other closed-minded elements in teaching, often invoke the concept of *considering* to suggest the ideal which they would wish to see realized. The following statement is typical of the way in which this idea occurs: "In their efforts to enable students to develop civic responsibility and judgement, schools should consider directly and openly the problems of contemporary society and should be free and encouraged to consider controversial issues, provided they do not espouse a partisan view or cause."[1] Here a distinction is drawn between *considering* an issue and *championing* a cause, and this will need to be examined shortly. But even if this distinction is accepted, the view advocated would not receive universal support. There are sizeable groups of parents and citizens who do not want pupils in schools (and some would extend this to universities also) even to *consider* certain issues. Regardless of the approach to be adopted, many prefer that, for example, certain topics which fall under "sex education" be excluded from the curriculum and the classroom altogether.[2] And as we have seen at the end of chapter 2, there are those who wish to prevent *other adults* from considering the views of those who are mistakenly believed to be advocating racism, for example. Students themselves have often made it impossible for other students to consider certain viewpoints on campus or in school.[3]

It is very important then that we examine carefully the objections which are, or might be, raised to the open consideration of issues in schools. Unless we do this, we cannot be sure that our view which favours open consideration can withstand critical scrutiny. It is necessary, however, to be clear before commencing, that the distinction (implicit in the quotation from the *Graham Report*) between considering and championing an issue is *not* accepted. It is rejected because the notion of considering is not itself violated if in the course of discussion the teacher attempts to defend a certain position. A person defending X can at the same time entertain objections to X, and in doing so is giving X his consideration. He is not merely putting X forward but is engaged in ongoing reflection about X, *as he defends X*. Similarly, as we saw in earlier chapters, believing that X is true does not rule out being open-minded about X.

Of course, it is at once obvious that if a teacher defends X, he *may* violate the concept of considering. He may refuse to look at any evidence or argument against X, or he may succeed in preventing his students from looking at X critically. When this happens, however, it is a result of his having championed X in a certain way, and not merely a result of his having defended X at all. The disappearance of the concept of considering in such a case is not a logical consequence of defending X, but is a consequence of defending X in a certain way. A teacher needs to calculate to what extent he can defend a particular position and still preserve the atmosphere of open-minded consideration.

It is a mistake to see "considering" as sharply distinct from "teaching," even though every act of considering is not an act of teaching. Still, considering is one of the forms which the polymorphous concept of teaching can take. If we deny this we falsely suggest that teaching always means something like "trying to persuade someone of a particular point of view," which to say nothing more ignores "teaching about." (I use the latter phrase to refer to the activity of teaching someone that certain matters are believed to be true, that certain claims are made by some people, without making any judgment about the accuracy or validity of the beliefs and claims. Of course, the teacher is maintaining that the beliefs are *held*, but he is not maintaining that the beliefs are true.[4] This remains an open question.) Alternatively, or additionally, we falsely suggest that considering necessarily rules out arguing for a particular position. We need to remember that teaching is a fuller notion than preaching, and that considering does not serve the ideal of neutrality but that of open-minded inquiry. In the service of this ideal, considering an issue and championing a cause need not be mutually exclusive. Considering as an activity of reflection involves giving something serious thought,[5] and there is no inconsistency in giving serious thought to that which we are defending.

3/   Objections to open inquiry

If we take considering to be consistent with defending a particular position, and proceed to advocate open discussion in which the teacher is permitted to defend particular positions provided that he does not violate the criteria of open-minded inquiry, then the number of objectors to our position greatly increases. It is time now to look at some of the points which are made against such open consideration of issues.

(a)   An objection might be based on the fact that sometimes a "consideration" implies that something has an important bearing on something else. That which is a consideration in this sense is something *worth* thinking about. Of course, it often turns out that that which is thought to be a consideration is in the end irrelevant. But the point of this objection is that when a teacher asks a student to consider something, it may be that a disguised and subtle evaluative judgment is being conveyed. It may *seem* as if the teacher is merely presenting a point for reflection, but *in effect* he or she is covertly saying: "This is important; you were neglecting this; this is worth thinking about, it changes the situation" and so on.

Insofar as this objection is opposed to teachers passing on their own evaluations uncritically, it commands the support of all those who favour open-minded teaching. It clearly violates the spirit of open consideration, precisely because the evaluations are made covertly and they are not exposed to the students' criticism. This objection then picks out a possible and potential fault in the consideration of issues, but it does not identify a necessary weakness. There is no reason in principle why teachers cannot make it clear *that* they are making an evaluation, and *why* they stand behind it. They can then encourage their students to think critically about it.

We do not need to conclude that teachers should not make evaluations *at all* because we are opposed to their being made in a certain way. It is an important part of the educator's task to *show* that and how one argument is more powerful than another as the arguments are being considered by the class. The emphasis here is on "show," however. It will not do, of course, if the teacher secures or attempts to secure conviction on the basis of authority-status.

(b) It is just possible, though I believe rather unlikely, that an exclusionist case might be based on the erroneous view that to be considering something, for example premarital sexual intercourse, is to be *inclined* to participate in that thing. The point to be made is that to give something careful thought does not mean or imply that one is prepared or disposed to do the action or to perform the behaviour in question. To consider it is, after all, to be weighing up the merits of doing *or* not doing it. Of course, we do not wish our children to be inclined to take dangerous drugs, for example, but this is not a reason for preventing them from considering the drug problem in the world. It would only be so if there were some evidence of an empirical kind that thinking about the drug problem caused a person to become inclined to take drugs. And there is, in fact, no evidence that this is so.[6]

(c)   While the above objection is perhaps unlikely, a related objection is much more commonly found. It is sometimes suggested that talk of considering an issue, with its connotation of serious and impartial reflection, implies an element of *uncertainty* about the issue, and that this is undesirable with respect to some issues. Thus for example, those who believe that premarital sexual relations are always immoral, may feel that if students even consider the whole question, it may suggest that there is something in the arguments of those who are in favour of premarital relations. The mere fact that the school spends time considering the case for, as well as the case against, will suggest that the pro-arguments have some merit. A number of comments are called for here. In the first place, we need to distinguish the accidental, contingent consequences of doing something and the necessary implications of doing that thing. It may be that considering an issue, i.e., reflecting on it, will in fact have the consequence of suggesting either that a certain argument is valid or that it has merit. This, however, is merely a further instance of the unintentional consequences of teaching which threaten any teaching-learning situation.[7] This is not at all a necessary implication of giving consideration to an issue, for we can reflect on arguments which we *know* to be invalid in order to better understand the error. Moreover, we need to distinguish between being worthy of attention, and being valid or plausible or desirable, etc. Immorality may be worthy of attention without being worthy of imitation. Finally, we need to remember that even if *we* believe that there is nothing to be said against a particular view we hold, as educators we cannot simply pass on our views uncritically. And if we are right in our views, we should have nothing to fear from an open discussion.

(d)   Having drawn the distinction, however, between being worthy of attention and being worthy of imitation, it might well be argued that there are surely some views that are just *not* worth attention or consideration in school. In a crowded timetable choices have to be made, and it is entirely reasonable that some issues should be judged less important than others. In this way it may be held that, for example, a certain person's poetry is not worth considering in literature classes.

It is true that some selection is necessary and desirable, though important questions remain to be answered about the right to make this selection. Does it rest with the students, the teachers, the school board or local authority, the parents, the local university or with none of these? Moreover, the judgment that X is *not* worth considering is curious in that it can only properly be made after consideration has been given. Before we can decide whether or not X has merit and warrants consideration by students in school, X must be given careful consideration. Any work initially deserves consideration, because in advance we cannot decide that it is without merit. X needs to be given serious attention if we are ever to decide that it does not deserve the serious attention of our students. The point of great significance for teaching which emerges here is that, however curricular decisions are arrived at, it is vital that the students grasp that there is no way of rationally determining that X is not worth considering in their literature classes other than the process of consideration itself. (Of course, this requirement of reason does not *in fact* prevent people from pronouncing on books which they have not read.) The danger of the hidden curriculum effect is enormous here, for students may well conclude that X is not important because it is not considered in school. They may come to this opinion, but it is not a considered one, if it is held uncritically as a result of the hidden curriculum. I believe that it would be a useful move in helping to offset this effect, if some books and works which are regarded by the educated community as shoddy and inferior were given consideration in schools. Students need to learn to make the relevant discriminations for themselves.

(e) It is not uncommon to encounter the views that there is not time to consider all positions and that consequently students should be presented with a "middle of the road" position. A recent contributor to the correspondence columns of the *Times Educational Supplement* managed to combine both of these when commenting on the perennial problem of treating *Genesis* in religious education classes: "The task of a county agreed syllabus, and of its religious education advisor, is presumably to see that the children are given, as far as possible, a consensus view from the middle bands, since this represents the balance of informed opinion and scholarship on this particular issue. In the limited time available for religious education in school, every minority view cannot be considered."[8] We noticed in looking at the fourth objection in this chapter that choices do have to be made in planning course content. But, as has often been pointed out,[9] to say that there is not enough time for X is to say that other things are more *important*. That is, there is a concealed value premise in this apparently factual remark. If our teaching is to be open-minded, our reason for regarding X as less important should be presented and be open for critical scrutiny.

The letter-writer in question does provide her criterion for exclusion, namely that X falls outside "the middle bands." X is, therefore, an *extreme* view, held only by a few, and does not represent the balanced judgment of informed scholarship. This position clearly reveals itself as an instance of what Antony Flew has recently labelled the "Truth-is-always-in-the-middle-Damper."[10] There is no reason in principle why the truth on a certain matter should be the position held by those in the middle. Indeed, as Flew has shown, the middle view can always be shifted by postulating a more extreme position, thus tugging the middle ground to one side. If our students are to consider issues seriously, they cannot be advised to make up their minds by trying to calculate what is the middle ground, or by counting the number of people in favour of a view. If a minority or extreme view is not to be considered in class, it must be because there is some *reason* to believe that it is false or confused *and* that greater educational value is to be derived by spending time on other views. Suppose, for example, that we identify three positions in a dispute as follows: (i) that X always causes Y; (ii) that X sometimes causes Y; (iii) that X never causes Y. Now clearly (ii) is the middle ground, but in spite of this, and even if 90 per cent of the academic community support (ii), either (i) or (iii) could be correct even though they have few defenders. If the advice of this contributor were followed, not only would minority views not be considered, the majority view would not be considered either, for it would be advanced on wholly irrelevant grounds. Irrelevant, that is, if it is the *truth* we are interested in, and not the question of how popular the view is. And, as I argued in chapter 3, in the educational context, our proper concern is with truth.

(f) It may at times be assumed that the activity of considering is undertaken in order to determine what we consider to be the case, i.e. what our considered opinion on some matter is. It will then be objected that this is inappropriate at times in schools because students are sometimes not in a position to determine what their considered opinion is. Insofar as this objection seeks to criticize those who force or persuade students to form an opinion before they can reasonably be expected to do so, it makes a valuable point.[11] But this does not constitute an objection to considering *as reflection*, for it is through reflection that we come to appreciate that we are *not* in a position to determine what our opinion is. After considering something, we are often obliged to say that we do not know *what to think*. Students can profitably consider disputed and pseudo-problems if it is recognized that the "I don't know what to think" response is legitimate. Reflecting in an open-minded way leaves it open whether or not a definite opinion will emerge.

(g) It is commonly urged that schools should not consider controversial matters because the students will only become confused. But to this it may be replied:

(i) Considering does not of course guarantee that we will achieve clarity, but there is no way of achieving clarity about issues without thinking about them.

(ii)   There is value in students coming to realize that they are confused, rather than falsely believing that they are clear about the issue. Considering an issue and remaining (or becoming) confused is the beginning of the elimination of the "false conceit of wisdom" which Socrates detected in the Sophists. Again we can make no firm recommendations for practice without having much more empirical evidence on how far certain states of confusion and puzzlement lead to boredom and a sense of futility, rather than to interest and a determination to pursue the puzzle.

Of course, in many subjects one can proceed a good way without getting into controversial matters, though in other subjects, like philosophy, one can barely begin. As one approaches the frontiers of a discipline, however, it becomes logically impossible to avoid such issues if one is to do anything that would warrant the description of continuing to work in the discipline. It is not, of course, logically necessary that controversy exist at the frontiers of a discipline, for it is logically possible for new theories to replace old ones without dispute. It is a fact, however, that this very rarely happens. Given the existence of such controversy, a student will have a distorted view of the discipline if he or she is led to believe that controversy does not exist.

(h)   The extreme relativism which was criticized in chapter 5 in connection with knowledge claims also occurs in discussions of value, and we may expect that opposition will be voiced to considering because, it will be alleged, to favour this is to beg the question in favour of a certain character-trait, namely considerateness. Such an objection might seem surprising, for it is tempting to hold that considerateness is one of those virtues which, as Hume put it, "sufficiently engages every heart, on the first apprehension."[12]

Still, there is room for a certain amount of disagreement. It may, for example, be held that some situations demand that we act inconsiderately, because other values take precedence. Or it may be pointed out that some people show too much consideration for others, and thereby encourage unwarranted interference by those others. Again, it may be held that some people do not deserve consideration or respect because, by their actions, they have forfeited this normal right.

The point which needs to be made in reply to these objections, however, is that a reasoned view on any of these points *demands* reflection. It is certainly true, for example, that serious disputes arise concerning how and when we are to act considerately, but advocating considering as reflection does not beg the answers to these questions. After open-minded consideration of the circumstances, we may agree that a certain person does not deserve respect, or that someone is showing too much consideration to another person. When a person is considering an issue, he has not made up his mind what to think about the issue, or he is rethinking a position previously formulated. Considering as reflection, then, entails an open-minded approach to such disputes. It is quite coherent, for example, to maintain that we consider that in these circumstances we need to act inconsiderately. It can be our considered opinion that we can show too much consideration. And the forms which considerateness should take are a proper matter for consideration.

(i) Our recent reference to Hume's writings on ethics will no doubt bring to mind his observation that in certain circumstances any particular value may be overshadowed by some other: "No quality, it is allowed, is absolutely either blameable or praiseworthy."[13] Hume pointed out, for example, how an intellectual trait like discretion, which is *almost always* valuable, might in some cases be a fault or an imperfection. In fact, as Hume describes discretion, it can be regarded as a form of considering as reflection. It is that quality "by which we carry on a safe intercourse with others, give due attention to our own and to their character, weigh each circumstance of the business which we undertake, and employ the surest and safest means for the attainment of any end or purpose."[14] But then, if considering is sometimes a fault, is it not the case that there are some objections to persuading students to consider issues? I believe that the solution here is not merely to emphasize Hume's point that "in the conduct of ordinary life, no virtue is more requisite," for this would not do justice to the exceptional cases. The point to be stressed is that it is *through* the process of considering that the nonabsolute value of considering can be appreciated. Hume offers, after all, what may properly be called "considerations" in support of his view, namely the examples of Cromwell and de Retz. Paradoxically, then, considering can lead to the realization that considering is not always of value. Similarly, we may find that a person is talking foolish nonsense and our open-mindedness does not demand that we continue to take him seriously. We may decide that it is nonsense, and are under no obligation to pay further attention unless we have some reason to believe that he may have started to talk sense.

We might find that the empirical consequences of considering issues in school were such that students became unable to detect those situations in which considering would be an imperfection. Or if able to recognize the situation, be unable to break their well-established habits. If we discovered such facts, we could, of course, attempt to offset such effects. And if we could find no way of doing this, we would have to decide whether or not the value of considering in the context of ordinary life outweighed the dis-value of the practice in the non-ordinary context. Since we are speaking of a practice which is *usually* valuable for *most* people (the Cromwells of this world and their special circumstances being genuinely rare), it seems that the calculations of utility would support the side of considering. In any case, those who object to students considering such issues as abortion in school could hardly appeal to this Humean point, because it is not the case that such issues call for precipitate decision-making. Students can be pondering such issues long before any overt action on their part is required at all.

It is worth pointing out here that we may on occasion judge it desirable to *postpone* criticism of a set of ideas. We shelve temporarily an open-minded examination of the beliefs in question. We may, for example, believe that we will not be in a position to make pertinent comments until we have listened to more of the arguments. But far from showing that we do not value open-minded inquiry, such a decision reveals how much we value it for it demonstrates that we do not wish to rush in with ill-formulated objections.

(j) A variety of related objections may be anticipated concerning, for example, the possibility of chaos and disturbances in classes which permit open discussion, or the alleged inability of teachers to deal with controversial issues in their classes. With respect to the question of disorder, it need only be said that there is no point in recommending open discussion if the conditions necessary for considering issues do not prevail. "Ought" implies "Can." We need to distinguish between objecting to open discussion and objecting to recommending open discussion in certain circumstances. It is here that serious empirical research is needed to uncover the sorts of conditions which may lead to chaos and disorder and to discover possible remedies.

If our teachers in the main cannot properly deal with controversial issues, we can plausibly maintain that this is a deficiency in their preparation, and argue that greater attention be given to this matter in courses of professional preparation. Of course, it will not normally be possible for a teacher to *resolve* an ongoing controversy—the resolution must wait on further researches by experts. But we can reasonably expect the teacher to be able to explain what the controversy involves and to begin to develop in the students the ability to assess the merits of the evidence as it is forthcoming.

Finally, as a word of caution, I would urge the reader to be wary about accepting certain arguments because they support certain policies which we happen to favour. We have already seen in chapter 4 how those who wish to indoctrinate students may yet favour the inclusion of ideas with which they disagree.[15] In the following extract a reason is offered for including controversial issues in the classroom and having them openly discussed:

People are willing to see the principle of debate practised in out-of-school institutions and even become an element in teaching and other activities, but they often take fright when they see discussion making its way into schools and universities. But to exclude politics from the school is to deny and contradict (as a principle and in practice) what people in general usually profess: that schools are a constituent of the *Polis*, the City, and that relationships between the two should be as close as possible.[16]

Leaving aside the question of how far people are *in fact* willing to accept debate in out-of-school situations, it is clearly unacceptable to base the desirability of discussion in school on the existence of discussion in society. On this view, there remains no independent argument for the importance of discussion in school, if the practice in society alters and debate in the *Polis* fades away or is destroyed.

Notes

Preface

1. James W. Trent and Arthur M. Cohen, "Research on Teaching in Higher Education," in Robert M. W. Travers, ed., *Second Handbook of Research on Teaching* (Chicago: Rand McNally, 1973), p. 1035.
2. Ibid., p. 1009.

Chapter 1

1. David Hume, *An Enquiry Concerning the Principles of Morals,* sec. VII.
2. John Stuart Mill describes the Emperor Marcus Aurelius as having had an "open and unfettered intellect." Incidentally, Mill's main point here is that *despite* his open-mindedness, Marcus Aurelius failed to see the value (from Mill's point of view) of Christianity. Hence Mill cannot be convicted of the mistaken view that the holding of certain specific beliefs is a necessary or sufficient condition of open-mindedness. See *On Liberty*, chap. 2.
3. Hume, *Enquiry Concerning the Principles of Morals*, sec. I.
4. I believe, though I cannot argue for this here, that trait-names of personality, such as dull, exciting, vivacious, boring, intriguing, mysterious, sombre, etc., involve assessment which is aesthetic or quasi-aesthetic in nature.
5. See my paper, "A mixed-form of the summary theory of character-traits defended," *The Personalist* LII, no. 4 (Autumn 1971): 750-54.
6. The categories of thinking discussed below are drawn from Alan R. White, *The Philosophy of Mind*, chap. 4.

7. See, however, the discussion in chapter 4 concerning beliefs which are held without evidence.
8. Karl Popper, *Unended Quest*, p. 38. "Utterly different" in the sense that it is a much *stricter* demand, and consequently rarer. Literally, it is the same attitude of open-mindedness, but satisfying this criterion normally puts one high on the scale.
9. Alan R. White, "Meaning and Implication," *Analysis* 32 (1971): 26-30.
10. Antony Flew, "Indoctrination and Doctrines," in I. A. Snook, ed., *Concepts of Indoctrination*, p. 81. This paper appeared originally as "What is Indoctrination?", in *Studies in Philosophy of Education* VI (Spring 1966): 281-306.
11. Lawrence Kohlberg, "Stages of moral development as a basis for moral education," in C. M. Beck, B. S. Crittenden, and E. V. Sullivan, eds., *Moral Education: Interdisciplinary Approaches*, p. 75.
12. H. Hartshorne and M. A. May, *Studies in the Nature of character* (New York: Macmillan, 1928-30).
13. Kohlberg, "Stages of Moral Development," p. 75.
14. In chapter 3 we will consider a different objection to the view that there is such a thing as open-mindedness. This is the objection, not as Kohlberg holds that the *facts* tell against the existence of such virtues, but that open-mindedness is logically impossible, i.e., ruled out *in principle*.
15. To see just *how* extraordinary the reasons can become, the reader is referred to the highly enjoyable and philosophically interesting novel by Roland Puccetti, *The Trial of John and Henry Norton* (London: Hutchinson, 1973.)

Chapter 2

1. Cf. Antony Flew, *Thinking about Thinking*, chap. 3. We will see below in chapter 4 that some would exclude certain people from the teaching profession because it is held that the beliefs which they are presumed to hold entail that they must be closed-minded.
2. Cf. chapter 1, section 7.
3. Descartes, *Rules for the Direction of the Mind*, II.
4. Aristotle, *Nichomachean Ethics*, bk. X.
5. D. J. O'Connor, *An Introduction to the Philosophy of Education*, p. 12.
6. John Dewey, *Democracy and Education*, p. 206.
7. See Karl Popper, *Unended Quest*, p. 79.

8. Cf. Israel Scheffler, *Science and Subjectivity*, p. 1.
9. Barry Feinberg and Ronald Kasrils, eds., *Dear Bertrand Russell . . .* (London: George Allen and Unwin, 1969), p. 108.
10. David Hume, *Enquiry Concerning the Principles of Morals*, Conclusion.
11. Descartes, *Discourse on Method*, sec. II.
12. See Popper, *Unended Quest*, p. 79.
13. Indeed Popper, who bitterly attacks dogmatism, says at one point, "Some degree of dogmatism is fruitful, even in science." Ibid., p. 42. We can, that is, *too easily* lose confidence in hypotheses as a result of a test. Combined with an auxiliary hypothesis, the original hypotheses might stand. On the other hand, it is odd for Popper to describe "the critical method" as that of "proposing bold hypotheses, and exposing them to the severest criticism, in order to detect where we have erred." Ibid., p. 86. "*Where*" suggests we have necessarily erred. Surely "*if*" would suit the open-minded approach better.
14. Joel Feinberg, "The Idea of a Free Man," in James Doyle, ed., *Educational Judgments*, p. 166.
15. See, for example, recent educational reports in Canada, such as *One Million Children* (CELDIC report, 1970) and *A Choice of Futures* (The Worth Report, Alberta, 1972). See also analytic philosophers such as Israel Scheffler, *Reason and Teaching* (Indianapolis: Bobbs-Merrill, 1973), p. 87. The popularity of the notion of commitment is indicated by R. S. Peters's remark about the person who produces his commitment "like the white rabbit producing his watch from his waistcoat pocket." See his "Concrete Principles and the Rational Passims," in Cornelius J. Troost, *Radical School Reform* (Boston: Little Brown, 1973), p. 216.
16. Too much should not be read into these labels. From another perspective what I call "logical" commitment may be called "rational."
17. BBC Radio talk, 1948. The text is reproduced in Bertrand Russell, *Why I am not a Christian* (London: George Allen and Unwin, 1957).
18. Elizabeth Edwards, "The Dedicated Teacher is the Teaching Profession's Greatest Enemy," reprinted in Clinton B. Allison, ed., *Without Consensus. Issues in American Education* (Boston: Allyn and Bacon, 1973), pp. 200-204.
19. Cf. also the discussion on "The limits of open-mindedness" in chapter 1, section 7.
20. Cf. R. S. Peters on "arbitrariness" in connection with the attempt to justify the value of justification. See R. S. Peters,

"The Justification of Education," in R. S. Peters, ed., *The Philosophy of Education*, p. 253.

21. I say "normally" because it may be that the *expectations* of others, based on their erroneous view that someone had made a commitment, could in certain circumstances create a commitment.

22. Hume, *Enquiry Concerning the Principles of Morals*, sec. V, note 1.

23. J. P. Corbett, "Teaching Philosophy Now," in R. D. Archambault, ed., *Philosophical Analysis and Education* (London: Routledge and Kegan Paul, 1965), p. 152.

24. John Dewey, *How we Think*, p. 177.

25. Descartes, *Letter from the Author* (to the translator of the *Principles of Philosophy*).

26. Plato, *Meno*, 84C.

27. See Jay F. Rosenberg, *The Practice of Philosophy: A handbook for beginners* (Englewood Cliffs: Prentice Hall, 1978), pp. 10-12.

28. Dewey, *Democracy and Education*, p. 206. To be fair to Dewey, he does say "child*like*."

29. Cf. Alan Montefiore, ed., *Neutrality and Impartiality: The University and Political Commitment*, p. 21.

30. Quoted in A. H. Armstrong, "Tradition, Reason and Experience in the thought of Plotinus," in *Accademia Nazionale Dei Lincei* (1974), p. 175.

31. I do not deal here with the underlying substantive issues in this letter, for example, the view that empirical claims concerning genetic inheritance imply, or are equivalent to, the immoral view that different races ought as such to be treated differently. These sorts of confusion have been very well exposed in Antony Flew, "The Jensen Uproar," *Philosophy* 48 (1973): 63-69.

32. For popular accounts see *Time*, June 20, 1977, and *Newsweek*, June 27, 1977.

Chapter 3

1. Jacques Barzun, *The American University*, p. 83.

2. Gordon W. Allport, *The Nature of Prejudice*, p. 20.

3. Allport, *Prejudice*, p. 20.

4. See chapter 1, section 6.

5. J. B. Bury, *A History of Freedom of Thought*.

6. Milton Rokeach, *The Open and Closed Mind*. Rokeach's empirical work is the more interesting and valuable because he has not neglected conceptual issues. Cf. "Our own view is that before we can explain a phenomenon, we must first know what it is we want to explain." Ibid., p. 11.

7. Joel Feinberg, *Social Philosophy* (Englewood Cliffs: Prentice-Hall, 1973), pp. 34-35.
8. Israel Scheffler, *The Language of Education*, p. 31.
9. Ibid., p. 21.
10. I am drawing here on the points made in Alan R. White, "Conceptual Analysis," in Charles J. Bontempo and Jack S. Odell, eds., *The Owl of Minerva* (New York: McGraw-Hill, 1975), pp. 103-17.
11. See in particular: Frederick Suppe, ed., *The Structure of Scientific Theories* (Urbana: University of Illinois Press, 1974); Stephen Toulmin, *Human Understanding*, vol. I (Oxford: Clarendon Press, 1972); Israel Scheffler, *Science and Subjectivity*; Thomas S. Kuhn, *The Structure of Scientific Revolutions* (Chicago: University of Chicago Press, 1962).
12. For a cautionary note against taking discovery by intuition to extremes, see Thomas Nickles, "Heuristics and Justification in Scientific Research: Comments on Shapere," in Suppe, *Structure of Scientific Theories*, pp. 571-89.
13. Carl G. Hempel, *Philosophy of Natural Science* (Englewood Cliffs: Prentice-Hall, 1966), p. 16.
14. For a detailed discussion of teaching methods and the idea of open-mindedness, see chapter 6.
15. Descartes, *Discourse on Method*, chap. 6.
16. Descartes, *Rules for the Direction of the Mind*, III.
17. Gilbert Ryle, *The Concept of Mind*, p. 17.
18. Allport, *Prejudice*, p. 24.
19. Ibid.
20. Basil Mitchell, "Reason and Commitment in the Academic Vocation," *Oxford Review of Education* 2, no. 2 (1976): 107. The concept of tenacity was discussed by Charles Peirce in "The Fixation of Belief," originally published in *Popular Science Monthly* (November 1877), and reprinted in Morris R. Cohen, ed., *Chance Love and Logic* (New York: Barnes and Noble, 1923), pp. 7-31.
21. Bryan Magee, *Popper*, pp. 23-24. Cf. also Popper's remarks cited in chapter 2, note 13.
22. Hempel, *Philosophy of Natural Science*, p. 30.
23. Karl Popper, *Conjectures and Refutations* (London: Routledge and Kegan Paul, 1963), p. 244.
24. An important exception is D. J. O.'Connor, *An Introduction to the Philosophy of Education*, pp. 11-12.
25. Rokeach, *Open and Closed Mind*.
26. Robert H. Thouless, *Straight and Crooked Thinking*, p. 144. An earlier statement of this view which links prejudice with a learned education can be found in *Three Dialogues* by the

eighteenth-century philosopher George Berkeley. In the third dialogue Philonous says: "I wish both our opinions were fairly stated and submitted to the judgment of men who had plain common sense, without the prejudices of a learned education." See Mary W. Calkins, ed., *Berkeley: Essay, Principles Dialogues* (New York: Scribner's, 1929), p. 309.

27. Thouless, *Straight and Crooked Thinking*, p. 166.
28. Cf. R. S. Peters, "Education as Initiation," in R. D. Archambault, ed., *Philosophical Analysis and Education* (London: Routledge and Kegan Paul, 1965), p. 96.
29. Contrast George F. Kneller, "Education and Political Thought," in George F. Kneller, ed., *Foundations of Education* (New York: John Wiley and Sons, 1963), p. 197.
30. Cf. Alan R. White, "On Claiming to Know," in A. Phillips Griffiths, ed., *Knowledge and Belief* (London: Oxford University Press, 1967), p. 110.
31. Paul H. Hirst, "Liberal Education and the Nature of Knowledge," in Archambault, *Philosophical Analysis*, p. 119.

Chapter 4

1. Donna H. Kerr and Jonas F. Soltis, "Locating Teaching Competency: An Action Description of Teaching," *Educational Theory* 24 (Winter 1974): 3-16.
2. R. S. Peters, ed., *The Role of the Head* (London: Routledge and Kegan Paul, 1976), p. 7.
3. It is sometimes held that teaching must *exhibit* or *display* what is to be learned; cf. P. H. Hirst and R. S. Peters, *The Logic of Education* (London: Routledge and Kegan Paul, 1970), p. 79. It may be that my example is not ruled out in their view because of their qualification, "if not overtly, at least by implication."
4. See Bernard Crick, "On Bias," *Teaching Politics* 1, no. 1 (1972): 3-12.
5. Alan Ryan, "Freedom," *Philosophy* XL (April 1965): 101.
6. *The Humanities Project: an Introduction* (London: Heineman Educational Books, 1970).
7. See his papers "Open-minded Teaching," *New Society*, July 24, 1969, pp. 126-28, and "Controversial Value Issues in the Classroom," in William G. Carr, ed., *Values and the Curriculum*, pp. 103-15.
8. Jean Rudduck, "The Humanities Curriculum Project," in *Dialogue*, Schools Council Newsletter, no. 22 (Spring 1976): 3-4.
9. Stenhouse, "Open-minded Teaching," p. 126.

10. Lawrence Stenhouse, "Neutrality as a Criterion in Teaching," in Monica Taylor, ed., *Progress and Problems in Moral Education* (Windsor, Berks: NFER Publishing Company, 1975), p.124.
11. See Stenhouse, "Controversial Value Issues," p. 106.
12. Stenhouse, "Neutrality as a Criterion," p. 125.
13. R. H. Ennis, "Is it impossible for the schools to be neutral?", in B. Othanel Smith and Robert H. Ennis, eds., *Language and Concepts in Education* (Chicago: Rand McNally, 1961), pp. 102-11.
14. Stenhouse, "Neutrality as a Criterion," p. 126.
15. Stenhouse, "Open-minded Teaching," p. 126.
16. Stenhouse, "Controversial Value Issues," p. 107.
17. Stenhouse, "Open-minded Teaching," p. 126.
18. P. T. Geach, "Good and Evil," *Analysis* 17 (1956-57): 33-42.
19. Rudduck, "Humanities Curriculum Project," p. 4.
20. Stenhouse, "Open-minded Teaching," p. 126.
21. Stenhouse, "Neutrality as a Criterion," p. 130.
22. Ibid.
23. Gajendra K. Verma and Barry MacDonald, "Teaching Race in Schools: Some effects on the Attitudinal and Sociometric Patterns of Adolescents," *Race* XIII, no. 2 (1971): 199.
24. Ibid.
25. See J. P. Parkinson and Barry MacDonald, "Teaching Race Neutrally," *Race* XIII, no. 3 (1972): 306, note f.
26. Arthur Bestor, *The Restoration of Learning* (New York: Alfred A. Knopf, 1955), p. 418.
27. For a detailed discussion of the fallacy see John Searle, *The Campus War*, pp. 189-90. This excellent philosophical study of educational problems has been unduly neglected.
28. Cf. ibid., pp. 190-91. In a contemporary Canadian case (see *Globe and Mail*, June 17, 1978, p. 8), involving a teacher who had written a tract alleging a Zionist conspiracy to seize control of the world, the local school board in question is reported to have taken the view that they could not act unless complaints were received about the teacher's *classroom performance*. This recognizes Searle's point—but see my comments at the end of section 4 of this chapter.
29. William McGucken, S. J., "The Philosophy of Catholic Education," in Nelson B. Henry, *Forty-First Yearbook of the National Society for the Study of Education*, p. 273.
30. See the earlier discussion in chapter 1, section 3, for an illustration of the logic of polymorphous concepts.
31. John Stuart Mill, *On Liberty*, chap. 2.

32. *The Christian Education of Youth,* Encyclical Letter of Pope Pius XI, "Divini Illius Magistri," 1929 (London: Catholic Truth Society, 1949), p. 43.
33. See Irving L. Janis, "Persuasion," in *International Encyclopaedia of the Social Sciences,* 12 (1968), 55-65.
34. John Wisdom, "Tolerance," in *Paradox and Discovery* (Berkeley: University of California Press, 1970), p. 140.
35. Descartes noted that men are commonly satisfied with their own measure of "good sense." See Descartes, *Discourse on Method,* chap. 1. We can also have a fond belief in our open-mindedness.
36. Contrast Brenda Cohen, "The Problem of Bias," in D. B. Heater, ed., *The Teaching of Politics* (London: Methuen Educational, 1969), p. 180.
37. Abraham Kaplan, "Values in Inquiry," in Gresham Riley, ed., *Values, Objectivity and the Social Sciences* (Reading, Mass.: Addison-Wesley, 1974), p. 87.
38. Alan Montefiore, ed., *Neutrality and Impartiality: The University and Political Commitment,* p. 33.
39. I. Scheffler, "Concepts of Education: Reflections on the Current Scene," in I. Scheffler, *Reason and Teaching* (London: Routledge & Kegan Paul, 1973), p. 61.
40. Ibid., p. 67.
41. See further my paper, "The Concept of Study," *Saskatchewan Journal of Educational Research and Development* 8, no. 2 (Spring 1978): 40-46.

Chapter 5

1. Milton Rokeach, *The Open and Closed Mind,* p. 5.
2. Discussion of this issue came to a head in Canada with the publication of *Religious Information and Moral Development,* Report of the Committee on Religious Education in the Public Schools of the Province of Ontario (Ontario: Department of Education, 1969). See also my paper, "The Mackay Report on Religious Education," *Teacher Education* no. 4 (Spring 1971): 16-23.
3. *Humanities for the Young School Leaver: An Approach Through Religious Education* (London: Evans/Methuen, 1969), p. 32.
4. *Schools Council Working Paper 36* (London: Evans Brothers, 1971), p. 91.
5. Lionel Elvin, "The Standpoint of the Secular Humanist," in A. G. Wedderspoon, *Religious Education 1944-1984* (London: George Allen and Unwin, 1966), pp. 177-78.
6. *Schools Council Working Paper 36,* p. 89.

7. See Kai Neilsen, "The very idea of a religious education," in *Journal of Education* (Nova Scotia) 2, no. 2 (Winter 1974-75): 36-38.

8. Elvin, "Standpoint," p. 177; cf. J. W. D. Smith, *Religious Education in a Secular Setting* (London: SCM Press, 1969), p. 69.

9. There is surely room for discussion of the *approach* to teaching if the injunction in *Matthew* 28:19 is followed.

10. Ninian Smart, *Secular Education and the Logic of Religion.* (London: Faber and Faber, 1968), p. 97; cf. C. Alves, *Religion and the Secondary School* (London: SCM Press, 1968), p. 186. (Alves, however, claims that the school *cannot* be neutral).

11. Elvin, "Standpoint," p. 177. On the concept of "teaching about," see below, chapter seven, section 2.

12. Elvin, "Standpoint," p. 170.

13. Howard Becker, "Whose side are we on?", reprinted in Gresham Riley, ed., *Values, Objectivity and the Social Sciences* (Reading, Mass.: Addison-Wesley, 1974), pp. 107-21.

14. Ibid., p. 116.

15. Gresham Riley, "Partisanship and Objectivity in the Social Sciences," in Riley, ed., *Values*, pp. 122-40. This critique makes a number of valuable points against Becker, but does not raise the criticisms which I deploy shortly.

16. Becker, "Reply to Riley's 'Partisanship and Objectivity'," in Riley, ed., *Values*, p. 142.

17. Riley, "Comments on Howard Becker's 'Reply'," in Riley, ed., *Values*, p. 145.

18. Becker, "Reply," p. 142.

19. Becker, "Whose side are we on?", p. 118.

20. Contrast Brenda Cohen, "The Problem of Bias," in D. B. Heater, ed., *The Teaching of Politics* (London: Methuen Educational, 1969), pp. 164-80. Though she sets out to make logical comments on bias, she writes that to talk about politics in neutral terms is "almost an impossibility." This can surely only mean that it is in fact very *difficult*: logical impossibilities are not a matter of "almost."

21. John H. Mueller, "Music and Education: A Sociological Approach," in Nelson B. Henry, ed., *Basic Concepts in Music Education* (Chicago: National Society for the Study of Education, 1958), p. 99.

22. Contrast Mueller, "Music and Education," p. 100.

23. Ibid., p. 103.

24. Ibid., pp. 102-3.

25. Ibid., p. 100.

26. Ibid.

27. Ibid., p. 101.

28. Ibid., p. 102.
29. P. H. Hirst and R. S. Peters, *The Logic of Education* (London: Routledge and Kegan Paul, 1970), p. 63.
30. See P. H. Hirst, "Liberal Education and the Nature of Knowledge," in R. D. Archambault, ed., *Philosophical Analysis and Education* (London: Routledge and Kegan Paul, 1965), pp. 113-38.
31. Descartes, *Rules for the Direction of the Mind*, III.
32. Michael F. D. Young, "An Approach to the Study of Curricula as Socially Organised Knowledge," in Michael F. D. Young, ed., *Knowledge and Control: New Directions for the Sociology of Education* (London: Collier-Macmillan, 1971), p. 23. Studies based on this general approach have now started to appear in Canada, e.g. Edmund V. Sullivan, *Kohlberg's Structuralism: A Critical Appraisal* (Toronto: Ontario Institute for Studies in Education, 1977). See my review in *CSSE News* IV:6 (March 1978): 11-12.
33. See Hirst and Peters, *Logic of Education*, p. 69.
34. Cf. Young, "An Approach," p. 23.
35. Ibid., p. 40.
36. Ibid., p. 23.
37. Ibid.
38. Hirst, "Liberal Education," p. 130.
39. Hirst and Peters, *Logic of Education*, p. 63.
40. Young, "An Approach," p. 40; cf. Young's further comments in "The Sociology of Knowledge," A Dialogue between John White and Michael Young, *Education for Teaching* no. 98 (Autumn 1975): 4-13, and no. 99 (Spring 1976): 50-58.
41. Antony Flew, *Sociology, Equality and Education*, pp. 22-23.
42. See note 35.
43. See "Sociology of Knowledge," p. 57; cf. Sullivan, *Kohlberg's Structuralism*, p. 10.
44. White and Young, "Sociology of Knowledge," pp. 51-52.
45. Antony Flew, *Sociology, Equality and Education*, p. 22.
46. Cf. note 43.
47. "Sociology of Knowledge," p. 58.
48. Ibid., p. 53.
49. Young, "An Approach," p. 33.
50. Hirst, "Liberal Education," p. 133.
51. Young, "An Approach," p. 36.
52. Ibid., p. 32.
53. Ibid., p. 33.

Chapter 6

1. Lawrence Stenhouse, *An Introduction to Curriculum Research and Development*, p. 25.

2. John McLeish, "The Lecture Method," in N. L. Gage, ed., *The Psychology of Teaching Methods* (Chicago: National Society for the Study of Education, 1976), p. 264.

3. Donald Bligh, *What's the Use of Lectures?* (London: University Teaching Methods Unit, 1971), p. 17.

4. Bligh, *What's the Use of Lectures?*, p. iii.

5. Norman E. Wallen and Robert M. W. Travers, "Analysis and Investigation of Teaching Methods," in N. L. Gage, ed., *Handbook of Research on Teaching* (Chicago: Rand McNally 1963), p. 481.

6. Ibid., p. 460.

7. Bligh, *What's the Use of Lectures?*, p. iii.

8. Lawrence Stenhouse, "Open-minded Teaching," *New Society*, July 24, 1969, p. 126.

9. Ibid.

10. R. S. Peters, "A recognisable philosophy of education," in R. S. Peters, ed., *Perspectives on Plowden* (London: Routledge and Kegan Paul, 1969), p. 18.

11. P. H. Hirst and R. S. Peters, *The Logic of Education* (London: Routledge and Kegan Paul, 1970), pp. 92-93.

12. Ibid., p. 101.

13. Cf. A. J. Ayer, *The Problem of Knowledge* (Harmondsworth: Penguin Books, 1956), p. 30.

14. See note 12.

15. See *Royal Commission on Education, Public Services and Provincial-Municipal Relations* (Halifax, Nova Scotia: Queen's Printer, 1974), vol. 3, chap. 58.

16. Ibid.; cf. my discussion in "Teacher Education and the Graham Report," *Journal of Education* (Nova Scotia) 2, no. 3 (Spring 1975): 5-6.

17. Ruth M. Beard and Donald A. Bligh, *Research into Teaching Methods in Higher Education* (London: Society for Research into Higher Education, 1971), p. 20.

18. Harold M. Schroder, Marvin Karlins, and Jacqueline O. Phares, *Education for Freedom* (New York: John Wiley and Sons, 1973), pp. 11-12.

19. Cf. Herbert Spencer's observation: "The suppression of every error is commonly followed by a temporary ascendancy of the contrary one." See *Education: Intellectual, Moral and Physical* (New York: D. Appleton, 1860), p. 102.

20. Ronald T. Hyman, *Ways of Teaching* (Philadelphia: J. B. Lippincott, 1970), p. 151.

21. Meredith D. Gall and Joyce P. Gall, "The Discussion Method," in Gage, ed., *Psychology of Teaching Methods*, p. 203.

22. D. Z. Phillips, "Democratization: Some themes in unexamined talk," *British Journal of Educational Studies* XXI, no. 2 (June 1973): 141.
23. Contrast Descartes' comment referred to in chapter 2, note 3.
24. I have discussed other aspects of the concept of listening in "Has listening had a fair hearing?", *Agora* 3, nos. 1 and 2 (Winter/Spring 1975-76): 3-13.
25. W. Warwick Sawyer, "Teaching or Research?", *University of Toronto Graduate* II, no. 3 (April 1975): 3-4.
26. See my paper, "The roles of teacher and critic," *Journal of General Education* XXII, no. 1 (April 1970): 43-44.
27. McLeish, "Lecture Method," p. 297.
28. Bligh, *What's the Use of Lectures?*, p. 5.
29. Wallen and Travers, "Analysis and Investigation," p. 481. Recent writers call for "new studies characterised by methodological rigour," implying that present research findings are not very reliable. See Gall and Gall, "Discussion Method," p. 198. Surprisingly, however, they do not raise such doubts about the methodology employed in connection with the research which tends to suggest that discussion is more effective than lecturing with respect to attitude change; cf. pp. 202-3. More recently still, researchers have raised doubts about the general significance of the comparative studies of lectures and discussion methods over the past forty years, suggesting that the results cancel one another out. See James W. Trent and Arthur M. Cohen, "Research on Teaching in Higher Education," in Robert M. W. Travers, ed., *Second Handbook of Research on Teaching* (Chicago: Rand McNally, 1973), pp. 997-1071 (in particular p. 1035).
30. Wallen and Travers, "Analysis and Investigation," p. 482.
31. Ruth Brandon, "Jehovah 1975," *New Society*, Aug. 7, 1969, pp. 201-2.
32. Ibid., p. 202.
33. Cited in Gall and Gall, "Discussion Method," p. 170.
34. Ibid., p. 203.
35. Ibid., p. 202.
36. Contrast John Walton, *Toward Better Teaching in the Secondary School* (Boston: Allyn and Bacon, 1966), p. 157.
37. Gall and Gall, "Discussion Method," pp. 202-3.
38. Beard and Bligh, *Research into Teaching Methods*, p. 47.
39. Cf. J. P. White, "Indoctrination," in R. S. Peters, ed., *The Concept of Education* (London: Routledge and Kegan Paul, 1967), p. 186.
40. Lawrence Stenhouse, "Controversial Value Issue in the Classroom," in William G. Carr, ed., *Values and the Curriculum*, p. 106.

41. Stenhouse has protested that "there is no implication in the
     project that teachers can in fact promote their own beliefs."
     This is correct for "almost insuperably difficult" does not mean
     "necessarily." But it is quite misleading for him to add that "it
     is enough that there should be uneasiness in the face of the
     possibility that they (i.e., teachers) may be able to do so."
     This is much weaker than "almost insuperably difficult." See
     Lawrence Stenhouse, "Neutrality as a Criterion in Teaching,"
     in Monica Taylor, ed., *Progress and Problems in Moral Education*
     (Windsor: NFER Publishing Company, 1976), p. 124. Cf. *The
     Humanities Project: An Introduction* (London: Heinemann Edu-
     cational Books, 1970), p. 7, where reference is made to the "in-
     escapable authority position of the teacher in the classroom."
     This, it is said, will "seriously limit the readiness of the student
     to consider other views."

42. A recent comprehensive review of the literature on discus-
     sion methods reports no such finding. Cf. Gall and Gall,
     "Discussion Method," pp. 166-216.

43. Ivan Illich, "The Alternative to Schooling," *Saturday Review*,
     June 19, 1971. But see my criticisms of Illich on this concept
     in my paper "Openness in Education," in Michael J. Parsons,
     ed., *Philosophy of Education 1974*, pp. 218-26.

44. S. J. Parnes and A. Meadow, "Effects of 'Brainstorming'
     instructions on creative problem solving by trained and
     untrained subjects," *Journal of Educational Psychology* 50
     (1959): 171-76.

45. John Dewey, *Democracy and Education*, p. 206. See also
     chapter 2, note 6 of this book.

46. Bligh, *What's the Use of Lectures?*, p. 175.

47. N. Miller and D. T. Campbell, "Recency and Primacy in Per-
     suasion as a function of the timing of speeches and measure-
     ments," *Journal of Abnormal and Social Psychology* 59 (1959):
     1-9.

48. Graham Nuthall and Ivan Snook, "Contemporary Models of
     Teaching," in Travers, *Second Handbook*, pp. 47-76.

49. Ibid., p. 71.

50. Ibid., p. 70.

51. See, for example, Mary Alice White and Jan Duker, *Education:
     A Conceptual and Empirical Approach* (New York: Holt,
     Rinehart and Winston, 1973), p. 109.

52. See, for example, the case given at the end of chapter 1, sec-
     tion 4. For an admirable statement on when and how refer-
     ence to an author's motives or character may be relevant, see
     Antony Flew, *Thinking about Thinking*, pp. 62-63.

53. See chapter 2, section 6 (b).

54. See chapter 5, section 3.

55. Nuthall and Snook, "Contemporary Models," p. 70.
56. Ibid., pp. 70-71.
57. Ibid., pp. 64-65.
58. Cf. I. Scheffler, *Science and Subjectivity*, pp. 86-87, on the notion of "acceptance."
59. Ruth Beard, *Teaching and Learning in Higher Education* (Harmondsworth: Penguin Books, 1970), p. 165.
60. Ibid.
61. See my paper, "The Concept of Study," *Saskatchewan Journal of Educational Research and Development* 8, no. 2 (Spring 1978): 40-46.

Chapter 7

1. *Royal Commission on Education, Public Services and Provincial-Municipal Relations* (Queen's Printer: Halifax, Nova Scotia, 1974), III: 132 (commonly referred to as the *Graham Report*). It is not entirely clear how "schools" is to be interpreted here. The point might be that the school as such should not support a particular cause. Or it might be that *teachers* within the school should not support particular causes. I suspect that the latter is intended, and this is the claim I wish to deal with. My arguments concerning the role of teachers cannot simply be extended to the school as an institution.
2. See, for example, John Eisenberg and Gailand MacQueen, *Don't Teach That!* (Don Mills, Ont.: General Publishing Company, 1972).
3. See John Searle, *The Campus War*.
4. Cf. I Scheffler, *The Language of Education*, p. 100.
5. It might be objected that if considering implied giving careful and adequate attention to issues, it would be superfluous to speak of giving "serious consideration" or "careful consideration," and yet these are very common expressions. The answer here is that (1) considering admits of degrees, and a person might want to stress that he would give of his *best* and (2) it is often necessary to spell out what ought to be taken for granted, just because people will say casually at times that they will consider X, and thus the proper strength of the notion becomes diluted.
6. Sometimes in ordinary speech we can convey that we intend to do something by saying, in a certain tone of voice, that we are considering X-ing. This is close to the device of litotes. And in some modern languages the word for "consider" can also mean "intend," cf. σκέπτομαι in modern Greek.

7. In contemporary discussion the "hidden curriculum" is the most famous instance. See Ivan Illich, "The Alternative to Schooling," *Saturday Review*, June 19, 1971.
8. *Times Educational Supplement*, 18 March 1977.
9. Cf. John Passmore, "On teaching to be critical," in R. S. Peters, ed., *The Concept of Education* (London: Routledge and Kegan Paul, 1967) p. 120, n. 15.
10. Antony Flew, *Thinking about Thinking*, pp. 44-46.
11. See, for example, some comments in my review of the Canadian Critical Issues Series (with Karen Duerden and Bruce Roald), *The History and Social Science Teacher* 10, no. 4 (Summer 1975): 5-11.
12. David Hume, *An Enquiry Concerning the Principles of Morals*, sec. II, pt. 1. In section VI, pt. 1, Hume lists "considerateness" as one quality which no person will deny to be a perfection.
13. Ibid., sec. VI, pt. 1.
14. Ibid.
15. See the discussion on "inoculation" techniques in chapter 4.
16. *Learning to Be. The World of Education Today and Tomorrow*, A report of the International Commission on the Development of Education (Unesco: Paris, 1972), p. 151.

Bibliography

Allport, Gordon. *The Nature of Prejudice*. Cambridge, Mass.: Addison-Wesley, 1954.

Barzun, Jacques. *The American University*. London: Oxford University Press, 1969.

Beck, C. M., Crittenden, B. S., and Sullivan, E. V. S., eds. *Moral Education: Interdisciplinary Approaches*. Toronto: University of Toronto Press, 1971.

Benn, S. I. "Universities, Society and Rational Inquiry," *The Australian University* 10, no. 1 (April 1972): 30-47.

Bury, J. B. *A History of Freedom of Thought*. London: Williams and Norgate, 1913.

Dewey, John. *How We Think*. London: D. C. Heath, 1909.

————. *Democracy and Education*. New York: Macmillan, 1930.

Feinberg, Joel. "The Idea of a Free Man," in James Doyle, ed., *Educational Judgments*. London: Routledge and Kegan Paul, 1973, pp. 143-69.

Flew, Antony. "What is Indoctrination?", *Studies in Philosophy and Education* VI (Spring 1966): 281-306.

————. "The Jensen Uproar," *Philosophy* 48 (1973): 63-69.

————. "Jensen: The Uproar Continues," *Philosophy* 49 (1974): 310-14.

————. *Thinking About Thinking*. Glasgow: Fontana/Collins, 1975.

————. *Sociology, Equality and Education*. London: Macmillan, 1976.

Hare, William. "The Mackay Report on Religious Education," *Teacher Education* 4 (Spring 1971): 16-23.

————. "Education Amid Cultural Diversity," *International Education* 2, no. 1 (Fall 1972): 36-44.

————. "Controversial Issues and the Teacher," *High School Journal* 57, no. 2 (November 1973): 51-60.

————. "The Concept of Discussion in Educational Theory," *Kansas Studies in Education* 23, no. 1 (Spring 1974): 6-12.

————. "Openness in Education," in Michael J. Parsons, ed., *Philosophy of Education 1974: Proceedings of the Thirtieth Annual Meeting.* Edwardsville: Studies in Philosophy and Education, 1974, pp. 218-26.

————. "Has Listening Had a Fair Hearing?", *Agora* III, nos. 1 and 2 (Winter/Spring 1975-76): 3-13.

————. "Considering," *Journal of Educational Thought* 9, no. 2 (August 1975): 107-14.

————. "The Open-Minded Teacher," *Teaching Politics* 5, no. 1 (January 1976): 25-32.

————. "The Concept of Study," *Saskatchewan Journal of Educational Research and Development* 8, no. 2 (Spring 1978): 40-46.

Henry, Nelson B., ed. *The Forty-First Yearbook of the National Society for the Study of Education Part 1: Philosophies of Education.* Chicago: University of Chicago Press, 1942.

Hollins, T. H. B., ed. *Aims in Education: The Philosophic Approach.* Manchester: Manchester University Press, 1961.

Kazepides, A. C. *The Autonomy of Education.* Athens: National Centre of Social Research, 1973.

MacNamara, D. R. "Sir Karl Popper and Education," *British Journal of Educational Studies* XXVI, no. 1 (1978): pp. 24-39.

Magee, Bryan. *Popper.* Glasgow: Fontana/Collins, 1973.

Manen, Max Van. "Teaching Open Mindedness," *History and Social Science Teacher* 12, no. 4 (Summer 1977): 250-56.

Mill, John Stuart. *On Liberty.*

Mitchell, Basil. "Reason and Commitment in the Academic Vocation," *Oxford Review of Education* 2, no. 2 (1976): 101-9.

Montefiore, Alan, ed. *Neutrality and Impartiality: The University and Political Commitment.* London: Cambridge University Press, 1975.

O'Connor, D. J. *An Introduction to the Philosophy of Education.* London: Routledge and Kegan Paul, 1957.

Peters, R. S., ed. *The Concept of Education.* London: Routledge and Kegan Paul, 1967.

————, ed. *The Philosophy of Education*. London: Oxford University Press, 1973.

Popper, Karl. *Unended Quest*. Glasgow: Fontana/Collins, 1976.

Reddiford, Gordon. "Rationality and Understanding," *Philosophy* 50 (January 1975): 19-35.

Rokeach, Milton. *The Open and Closed Mind*. New York: Basic Books, 1960.

Ryle, Gilbert. *The Concept of Mind*. Harmondsworth: Penguin Books, 1963.

Scheffler, Israel. *The Language of Education*. Springfield: Charles C. Thomas, 1960.

————. *Science and Subjectivity*. Indianapolis: Bobbs-Merrill, 1967.

Scriven, Michael. "The Values of the Academy," *Review of Educational Research* 40, no. 4 (October 1970): 541-49.

Searle, John. *The Campus War*. Harmondsworth: Penguin Books, 1972.

Snook, I. A., ed. *Concepts of Indoctrination*. London: Routledge and Kegan Paul, 1972.

————. "Neutrality and the Schools," *Educational Theory* 22, no. 3 (1972): 278-85.

Stenhouse, Lawrence. "Open-minded Teaching," *New Society*, July 24, 1969, pp. 126-28.

————. "Controversial Value Issues in the Classroom," in William G. Carr, ed., *Values and the Curriculum*. A report of the Fourth International Curriculum Conference. Washington: National Education Association Publications, 1970, pp. 103-15.

————. *An Introduction to Curriculum Research and Development*. London: Heinemann, 1975.

Thouless, R. H. *Straight and Crooked Thinking*. London: Pan Books, 1974.

————. "Rationality and Prejudice," T. B. Davie Memorial Lecture. Cape Town: University of Cape Town, 1964.

White, A. R. *The Philosophy of Mind*. New York: Random House, 1967.

————. "Meaning and Implication," *Analysis* 32 (1971): 26-30.

————. "Conceptual Analysis," in Charles J. Bontempo and S. Jack Odell, eds., *The Owl of Minerva*. New York: McGraw-Hill, 1975, pp. 103-17.

White, John and Young, Michael. "The Sociology of Knowledge," *Education for Teaching* 98 (1975): 4-13, and 99 (1976): 50-58.

Index